Being my best in Your service

My character is forged by my choices. You will see it in my manner and my manners. You will see it in my confident optimism. It is how I stand and talk and laugh and listen. I seek to do what is right rather than what is personally advantageous. Lord, let me not rest upon what I have done but challenge me to see what I still can do. Give me the strength to be brave and to keep trying. Following my Catholic faith, I strive to become the best person that I can be in Your service.

Give me work to do.
Point me to my neighbor in need.
Choose me to go first or last.
Take me as the example.
Depend upon my honor.

I ar  ion®.

D1299898

Catholic Evangelism

"Go and make disciples of all nations, baptizing them in the name of the Father, and of the Son, and of the Holy Spirit, teaching them to observe all that I have commanded you and I am with you always, even unto the end of the world." – Matthew 28:19-20

We, the laity, comprise 98% of the Catholic Church. Through our prayers and our example, we must assume the major responsibility for reform and growth in the Church while giving full support and obedience to our clergy.

We can use these pocket-sized *Catholic Action Principles*® as a non-intrusive catalyst to create positive conversations at home, at work and in society. Share these books with your family, friends, neighbors, co-workers and students. Your generosity will be respected and appreciated.

Companies, schools, colleges and organizations who are interested in reaching a wide Catholic audience are welcomed to inquire about advertising in future printings of this book. Also, footnotes may be added to pages to memorialize a loved one. To learn more about these sponsorship opportunities, please visit CatholicActionPrinciples.com.

The Catholic Action Principles™

By Bill FitzPatrick

Educational and motivational materials from the American Success Institute are available at special discounts for bulk purchases. For additional information, contact:

American Success Institute
5 North Main Street, Natick, MA 01760

www.success.org • e-mail: info@success.org

Phone: 508-651-3303

Cover, book design, typography, and electronic pagination by Painted Turtle Productions, Newton, MA. www.paintedturtle.com

Printed in the United States of America

ISBN 1-884864-20-1
Library of Congress Number: 2004112278

Table of Contents

THE 100 ACTION PRINCIPLES®:

About The Catholic Action Principles™

What is so inviting about the tried and true advice of *The Catholic Action Principles™* is that the beneficial results are immediate. Just stop, take a few deep breaths, read for a moment and think. You can change your life for the better in an instant. You can make an immediate decision to become more aware of how you are living your life and recognize your personal choice to be happy. Guided by your Catholic faith, you can make positive decisions and take appropriate actions. You can listen more, smile more, be more patient and volunteer more often. You can take the lead and be in control. You can choose to be a better partner, parent, friend, son, daughter, employer, employee and citizen. In short, you have the God given power to choose a life of self-improvement and a commitment to helping others. And, no one can take this power from you. You can live an active life and be successful, happy and at peace.

The tone of *The Catholic Action Principles™* is motivational. These Action Principles® are for you, a self-reliant take-charge person of action willing to study and work hard for yourself, your family, your community and the greater glory of God.

Allow the Catholic Action Principles™ to serve as inspirational guides to reinforce your Catholic value system. The intent is to challenge and stimulate your thinking as you create your own independent success philosophy formalized in your daily action plans, your to-do list.

In addition, the Catholic Action Principles™ can serve as a catalyst to initiate faith-based discussion on a broad range of everyday life issues. Each of the Action Principles® presents an opportunity for a group leader to direct conversation to a faith-based course of practical common sense action. This positive dialogue could take place between parent and child, teacher and student, counselor and client, manager and employee in groups or classes or in prayerful solitary meditation. The intended result is for individuals to discover for themselves that living the Catholic faith is not spending one hour in Church on Sunday morning but rather a joyous way to live 24/7, 168 hours a week. It is a proudly proclaimed and actively lived Catholicism.

Bill FitzPatrick

PREFACE

VERY REVEREND DAVID M. O'CONNELL, C.M. PRESIDENT, CATHOLIC UNIVERSITY OF AMERICA

Be Great for the Greater Glory of God

We grow by dreams. Significant people are all dreamers. *"To the greater glory of God"* there may be among you the great dreamer and the great dream. In your quiet time, as you pray, your potential for earthly greatness will become apparent to you.

REVEREND DAVID M. O'CONNELL

You may be the great researcher who finds the cure for AIDS or cancer. You may be the great social worker who discovers how to provide homes for the homeless and a quality of life for the poor that will end their poverty. You may be the great priest or religious who preaches and ministers the Gospel in such a way that the new evangelization proclaimed by Pope John Paul II becomes a reality. You may be the great athlete who sets new records that will inspire others to pursue physical health and well being. You may be the great lawyer whose pursuit of justice ennobles the profession in ways unimagined before. You may be the great politician, the great policeman or the great poet. You may be the great educator who touches young lives in the way that his has been touched right here. You may be the great husband, the great father or the great friend and neighbor whose great love and compassion bring healing and wisdom and peace to his family and community – great dreamers, great dreams all with the great theme, *"to the greater glory of God."*

As you endeavor to improve yourself and help others, use these Action Principles® as seeds for thought and discussion. Challenge yourself to live your Catholic faith as a person of action motivated to work on behalf of your family, friends, co-workers and neighbors. Then, allow your success, your strength and compassion to reach out to the elderly, the homeless, the illiterate, the needy and the victims of injustice. Give it all away, in Christ's name. Proceed with confidence. God is with you. Do your best. You will feel good. You will be happy.

✝

POPE JOHN PAUL II

Imitate the Good Samaritan

What makes a volunteer dedicate his/her life to others? First of all, the innate movement of the heart that inspires every human being to help his fellow man. It is a law of existence. A volunteer experiences a joy that goes far beyond what he has done when he succeeds in giving himself freely to others.

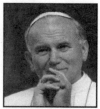

POPE JOHN PAUL II

Wherever situations of hardship and suffering appear, manifest the hidden resources of dedication, goodness and heroism which dwell in the heart of the human person.

Continue your journey with courage; do not let difficulties ever stop you. May Christ, the Good Samaritan, be the sublime model to be imitated by every volunteer. Imitate Mary who, by going "in haste" to assist her cousin Elizabeth, became a messenger of joy and salvation. May she teach you her humble and concrete charity and obtain from the Lord the grace for you to recognize him in the poor and suffering.

Dear Brothers and Sisters who make up this "army" of peace spread over the face of the earth, you are a sign of hope for our times. With these wishes, I impart a special Apostolic Blessing to you, and all whom you meet every day in the course of your service to the human person.

Most Reverend Charles J. Chaput, O.F.M. Cap.
Archbishop of Denver

Remember the Little Things

St. Augustine once said, *"to be faithful in little things is a big thing."* Devotion to family sounds like a simple thing, and it is. Gratitude, humility, faithfulness – these all are simple things. They're also very difficult. It's easy to talk about fixing the problems of American society with big national programs and policies, because we can always blame somebody else when they don't work.

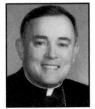

ARCHBISHOP
CHARLES J. CHAPUT

Personal change, personal moral integrity, personal fidelity to people and principles – that's much harder work, because we're stuck with the clay of who we are, and there's nobody to blame but ourselves if we fail. But in persisting in these little things, we accomplish a big thing. We affect others. One life, lived well, can begin to change the world.

A reporter once asked Mother Teresa the secret of her success. She answered that she wasn't called to succeed, but only to try. Success was God's business. Trying was her business. She wasn't called to find big solutions to poverty, but to live the little solution of personal love that would become a good infection in the hearts of other people. ✝ *14* ✝

HIS EMINENCE ANTHONY CARDINAL BEVILACQUA, J.CD., J.D.
ARCHBISHOP EMERITUS, PHILADELPHIA

Live With Integrity

Integrity may be defined as personal honesty. People of integrity live by a code of values. They are truthful with themselves and others. But, the world offers many temptations for people to compromise their integrity for personal gain and profit. It can happen to anyone.

ANTHONY CARDINAL
BEVILACQUA

There are many benefits to being completely honest. You will view the world in a brand new way. Your relationships will be based on trust rather than suspicion. You will be a good example to your children and your friends. When you are successful, the praise you receive will feel even greater because you followed your principles and honored your values.

Personal honesty may not be popular today; but, if you try to be honest in all your affairs, you will be at peace with yourself, with others, and with God. You will live with integrity.

†

His Excellency John Clement Favalora, D.D., S.T.D.
Archbishop of Miami

Find Security In God

We, as Americans, are experiencing the fear and uncertainty that most other countries in the world live with daily. There are countries beset by civil war. There are countries numbed by decades of terrorist acts. Where will we find security in this uncertain world? In one person alone: God. Jesus is the one certainty in our uncertain world. He is the way, the truth and the light.

Archbishop John Clement Favalora

Our faith should not be in gas masks or duct tape. Our faith should be in God. He alone can save us. He alone has promised us an afterlife without violence, without strife, without death. To him alone should we turn in our hour of need.

I firmly believe that God does listen to our prayers. So I would ask that you redirect your energies: Spend time in prayer. Many parishes have added rosaries, perpetual adoration and Masses for peace to their schedules. Find out which is nearest to you and stop by. Or make it a point, sometime during the day, to pause briefly and say a prayer. God is with us always. He alone can save us. May he hear our prayers.

His Eminence Edward Cardinal Egan, D.D., J.C.D.
Archbishop of New York

See God's Image In Everyone

Edward Cardinal Egan

May we tolerate discrimination because of race or creed? May we accept the poverty of others as something unrelated to ourselves? May we allow the sick and disabled to be neglected? May we stand idly by while the being within the mother is killed, even though no one has ever been able to prove that it is other than a human being with an inalienable right to live? May we look the other way when the elderly are put to death because someone questions the quality of their life?

To all of these questions, the answer must be a resounding no. And the reason is crystal clear. The victim of discrimination, the impoverished, the sick, the disabled, the unborn, the elderly, are all images of God, mirrors held up to divinity, beings for whom a God would and did die. There can be no genuine faith if there be wavering regarding the rights of those images of divinity.

Observe Your Actions

A principle that I learned a while ago in philosophy class is, *"Action follows being."* The perennial quest for understanding *"who I am"* can be answered very easily by observing one's actions. I wonder, *"How would someone describe me after observing me for a week?"* Would anyone know that I am a follower of Christ after watching my footsteps?"

DR. MARGARET
MARY FITZPATRICK

The fundamental commandment to *"love God and one's neighbor"* has to lead us in our decision-making each day. Whether it is how we are using the earth's resources, how we care for children and the elderly, or how we define who is our neighbor, in these actions we are defining ourselves.

Being proactive and reflectively open to opportunities are two important stances in this journey of becoming a Christian. Trying to do and be as Christ would have us, is saying, *"I love you"* to those lives we touch.

We are each uniquely beautiful and gifted. To be our best selves is such a great gift to the world.

Watch out world, here I come!

HIS EMINENCE ADAM CARDINAL MAIDA, J.C.L., J.D., S.T.L.
ARCHBISHOP OF DETROIT

Accept The Challenges of Peace and Freedom

The Holy Father reminds us that there will be no peace in the world unless there is justice within every nation and among all the nations of the world. Secondly, there will be no justice unless the dignity of all life is respected. We are challenged to protect the dignity of every human life from the first moment of conception

ADAM CARDINAL MAIDA

until last natural breath. We are challenged to respect the dignity of the stranger and the migrant.

From the words and example of the Lord Jesus and His mother, we can come to a new appreciation of the great gift of freedom we enjoy in our country – a freedom that brings with it a commitment to share our gifts and talents and to be faithful in all of our relationships, a freedom that challenges us as individuals and as a nation to be concerned about the rights of all people everywhere and the building-up of the common good.

✝

SISTER MARY ROSE McGEADY, D.C.
PRESIDENT AND CEO OF THE COVENANT HOUSE

Let Your Voice Be Heard

Let us all strive to honor God by serving as a voice for the voiceless of society, for those whose cries for help go unheard. There is an enormous gap to be bridged between the youth of the streets and the people in power whose decisions directly affect their young lives. We must make the empowered aware of this

SISTER MARY ROSE McGEADY, D.C.

enormous gap. The world of our homeless children is based on survival. Each day they find themselves overcome with fears about whether they will have something to eat or a place to sleep.

Please know that each of you has a voice that must speak loudly and cry out for justice. Our children are counting on us, for they have been let down too often in their short existence here on earth. Do not be intimidated by this responsibility; it is a blessing to be in a position to help another. The only way we can fail is to stop using our voices on behalf of the voiceless. The same God who asks that we show absolute respect and unconditional love for his children also asks that we strive for justice and mercy. Let your voice be heard.

MOST REVEREND HARRY J. FLYNN, D.D.
ARCHBISHOP OF ST. PAUL AND MINNEAPOLIS

Choose Life

Our Catholic moral teaching has always recognized the responsibility of government to protect citizens from persons who might be dangerous and harmful to others. This teaching has allowed the death penalty for particularly heinous crimes when the criminal is a continued threat to others. However, we must guard against a growing acceptance of revenge as a principle of justice. The alternative to the death penalty is life imprisonment without parole.

ARCHBISHOP HARRY J. FLYNN

The Gospel kingdom of peace and justice is built on a foundation of love that is capable of compassion and mercy. We must believe in the all-powerful redemptive love of God, which can change hearts, convert people, and renew all things. We must be a people committed to hope for those who seem to be hopeless.

If we are pro-life, we cannot support the death penalty. All life needs to be upheld as sacred and gifted by God, from life in the womb to the life of a convicted criminal. We must affirm all life. We must believe in the sacredness and the dignity of every human life, even the lives of those who have committed terrible crimes. We must choose life.

REVEREND JAMES J. MAHER, C.M.

Cross Over

By his own admission, early in his life St. Vincent de Paul was an ecclesiastical climber. He was well on his way toward climbing up the institutional ladder in the Roman Catholic Church. One day, while hearing the confession of a person who was poor, St. Vincent was overtaken by his authentic priestly vocation, to serve Jesus Christ in the poor. He "*crossed over*" to the world of the poor. Today his legacy is rooted in his service to the poor and the church but the core of his life and sanctity was his willingness to answer God's call to "*cross over*" to the world of the poor and suffering.

REVEREND JAMES J. MAHER, C.M.

The same God who called St. Vincent to "*cross over*" to the world of the poor calls to us today. Ask for the gift of faith to "*cross over*" to the poor, the suffering, and those who live in material, social and spiritual isolation. When we have the courage to "cross over" into these uncomfortable worlds and to be changed, we will resonate with the life of St. Vincent and the abundance of life in Christ Jesus.

✝

DR. MONIKA K. HELLWIG
THEOLOGIAN

Stand And Be Heard

Prayer creates the opportunity for us to evaluate our actions by the guidance of the Holy Spirit, and work toward an attitude of detachment from self-interest in making decisions, and trying to enter into the mind and intentions of Jesus. With a confidence born of our Catholic values and an attitude tempered by humility, we are prepared

DR. MONIKA K. HELLWIG

to create initiatives that help us battle and deal with life's difficulties. We can find peace, secure in our faith that God reaches out to all people at all times.

Empowered by the grace of God, we can and must stand and let our voices be heard. We must never take for granted wars; poverty; famines; injustices; margination of ethnic, racial, linguistic, or economic groups; or other unnecessary sufferings or deprivations. We must never acknowledge a separation of politics and economics from religious values and judgments. In the spirit of Ignatius of Loyola, with courtesy, courage, endurance and self-control, we embrace a vigorous, optimistic, world-affirming spirituality, committed to God's service.

✝

Become A Knight

The Catholic family communicates the moral way of life that consists in following Jesus. Through faith, the Catholic family becomes a special communion of persons on a journey with him, a journey that is both moral and personal. The role of parents in leading the Catholic family is to educate their children in the Catholic way of life.

MR. CARL ANDERSON

The Knights of Columbus knows this truth. It is one reason why family activities throughout the year are so important. Activities such as corporate communions, rosaries and family picnics all highlight the special fraternity and the special community to which the Catholic family is called. These activities strengthen the bonds that hold families together at a time when too many social forces work to loosen them. They help create a strong and positive sense of Catholic identity among our children at a time when many social forces work to blur distinctions between believers and the larger, secular society.

Family participation in our many Knights of Columbus family-centered activities is one of the best ways to foster the type of Catholic identity that will enable our youth to make the tough moral decisions society is forcing upon them in a way consistent with Church teaching. Join us in celebration of faith, family and fraternity.

MOST REVEREND DONALD W. WUERL, S.T.D.
BISHOP OF PITTSBURGH

Speak And Live The Faith

Imagine what the world would be like if every baptized Catholic accepted the challenge to share the faith with every other person and to live out the call to holiness wherever he or she might be — in the midst of the family, at work, in the public sector — wherever we live and work and experience God's grace.

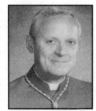

BISHOP DONALD W. WUERL

Each of us must be a force for the Gospel in our sphere of life. The voice and activity of the laity will ultimately determine the direction of society. The voice of Catholic physicians needs to be heard in the area of medicine. Catholic lawyers need to speak out on the ethics involved in the practice of the law. Catholic parents should be involved in education issues. Each of us must be a force for the Gospel in our sphere of life. In our lands where increasingly we see the arrogant claim of secularism to be the only true expression of national ideals and goals, the voice of committed Catholics is all the more necessary. It is the task of each layperson to speak and live the faith today.

MOST REVEREND ROBERT E. MULVEE, D.D., J.C.D.
BISHOP OF PROVIDENCE

Take The Peace Pledge

**BISHOP ROBERT
E. MULVEE**

Join your heart with mine and pledge to continue through prayer, fasting, reflection and action our non-violent journey in response to Jesus' call to be hopeful and blessed peace-makers. Making peace must start with-in ourselves as we commit to becom-ing nonviolent and peaceable people:

To respect myself, to affirm others and to avoid uncaring criticism, hateful words, physical attacks and self-destructive behavior.

To share my feelings honestly, to look for safe ways to express my anger, and to work at solving problems peacefully.

To listen carefully to one another, especially those who disagree with me, and to consider others' feelings and needs rather than insist on having my own way.

To apologize, make amends, to forgive others, and to keep from holding grudges.

To treat the environment and all living things with respect.

To promote athletic and recreational activities that encour-age cooperation and to avoid social activities and entertain-ment that make violence look acceptable.

To challenge violence in all its forms whether at home, at school, at work, in the parish or in the community, and to stand with others who are treated unfairly.

✝

Perform Random Acts of Kindness

The two basic commandments given us by Jesus are love of God and love of neighbor. Service is another way of saying, *"love of neighbor."*

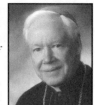

BISHOP ROBERT J. BANKS

Love is the best way for a heart to change. We know how much God loves each one of us and how good God has been to each one of us. Hopefully, our appreciation of God's love inspires us to serve. Service makes us think of other people, not just ourselves. That kind of thinking is at the heart of the Gospel.

Each parish, household and individual is encouraged to come up with at least one random act of kindness every week. It can be to a stranger, a neighbor, a family member or whoever comes to your mind. It is our hope that every parishioner will think of some way in which he or she can or does reach out in kindness to someone else. Cutting the grass for an elderly neighbor or baking cookies for the children next door would fit. Let's all do it!

✝ 27 ✝

✝

MOST REVEREND JOHN J. MYERS, J.C.D., D.D.
ARCHBISHOP OF NEWARK

Carry On

For us to be true disciples of Jesus Christ, we must follow His commandment of love. We must love one another, help and support one another. But this does not mean some weak or amorphous way of life. Jesus told us, *"You will remain in my love if you keep my commandments."*

**ARCHBISHOP
JOHN J. MYERS**

The Way is not of our making or our design. It is a Way designated by the Lord Jesus and proclaimed by His Church across the centuries. It is a way of goodness and honesty, founded in the truth of God's creation. But also, it is a way of the cross. It is a way of joy when the truth is embraced and lived. It is a way the Lord has chosen for us that we may abide in His love. It is a way which will find us walking with the Blessed Virgin Mary and all the saints because we seek the gift of loving one another in His name.

No matter how dark the sky, no matter how bleak the outlook, no matter how weak we feel in the face of terrible problems, the grace of Jesus Christ is sufficient for us to carry on. And we shall.

HIS EMINENCE JUSTIN CARDINAL RIGALI, J.C.D.
ARCHBISHOP OF PHILADELPHIA

Go And Serve With Love

Every time we are sent forth from Mass we are sent out on a mission – a mission to love and serve the Lord. We love and serve our Lord through our stewardship. Our reward for stewardship is peace.

JUSTIN CARDINAL RIGALI

When Jesus found the Apostles hiding in fear on the first Easter night, he said to them, *"Peace be with you. As the Father has sent me, so I send you."* He sent them out to do the work of the Father.

In today's hectic world, we spend too much time striving for material possessions, fame and power and not enough time striving for positive relationships with one another. We must humbly follow Jesus. There we will find peace and love.

Everything we have and everything we are is a gift from God. Everything we have is enough. This simple realization frees us from the craziness of always striving for more. When we share our gifts with others and return a portion of them to the Lord, then we are fulfilling the purpose for which God made us and blessed us. In all these ways we find peace. Your gift of time, talent and treasure helps do God's work in our parishes and beyond.

✝

Witness, Worship and Serve

All Christians are configured to Christ through baptism, for that is the sacrament by which we are incorporated into the Church, participate in Christ's death and resurrection, and assume the name *"Christian."* All Christians are called to a life of discipleship and are to extend his work and presence in the world today. All share in the one same vocation – to be the Body of Christ, building up the Kingdom of God through witness, worship, and service.

ROGER CARDINAL MAHONY

The baptized serve God through administration, feeding the hungry, caring for the needs of the sick, working for justice, washing the feet of the homeless, safeguarding and protecting the rights of the last, the littlest, and the least, giving the Body and Blood of Christ to those gathered at the Table of the Lord, and bringing this Holy Communion to those who are sick at home or in hospital.

At the core of our ongoing renewal is this key insight: God is best glorified when the greatest number of people participate to the fullest degree possible in the mission of Christ and Spirit through witness, worship, and service.

✝

HIS EMINENCE THEODORE CARDINAL MCCARRICK, PH.D., D.D.
ARCHBISHOP OF WASHINGTON, D.C.

Reach Out To Your Neighbor

We speak of making a difference in the world, and every one of you in your heart of hearts is hoping that you will find your way to do that. Whatever it is, it must be something which reaches out to the poor, the needy, to the newcomer, the stranger, to the confused and to those who need help. If you want to

THEODORE CARDINAL
MCCARRICK

be fully human and fully alive, you have to be aware of your neighbor and your neighbor's needs. You have to be willing to reach out to that neighbor in love, in grace and in generosity.

Never become provincial. Never become isolationists. Never become so wrapped up in your own self that you become unaware of the challenges and greatness and wonder of the rest of the world. Change the world. Don't forget the poor. Don't forget that what you do affects every corner of this globe. Don't forget that perhaps the greatest lesson is that God watches us and loves us and reaches out into our lives to make a difference, so that you and I may make a difference too.

✝

Practice Forgiveness

The practice of forgiveness is at the heart of the Church's work to spread the Gospel. The Church's preaching of God's forgiveness explains her constant preoccupation with respect for human life, from conception to the moment of natural death. Forgiveness restores life; hatred brings death.

FRANCIS CARDINAL
GEORGE

There are times in a person's life when forgiveness may seem impossible. Forgiveness is a personal decision to go against the natural instinct to pay back evil with evil. It goes beyond pardon to the giving up of resentment. The offer to forgive is necessary for healing and peace; the preaching of forgiveness, from God and for one another, is central to the Church's mission in the world.

From the cross, Jesus shows us the conditions which enable us to forgive. To the hatred with which his persecutors nailed him to the cross, Jesus responds by praying for them. He not only forgives them, he continues to love them, to want their good, to intercede for them. Only forgiveness from the heart can release us from our own hurts and misery and free us to share Christ's gifts with others.

His Eminence Sean Patrick O'Malley, O.F.M. Cap.
Archbishop of Boston

Stand Firm

Jesus came into our world to reveal the merciful face of the Father. In a world of suffering and violence, of injustice and pain, the love and mercy of our God is made manifest to us in Jesus. We who are his church are called to carry on these tasks in today's world. As God's pilgrim people, we struggle to

Archbishop Sean Patrick O'Malley

advance the mission that he has entrusted to us, in spite of our shortcomings, in spite of our unworthiness.

If we are a praying people when we gather at the Eucharist, we will know God's language and be a part of the miracle of self-giving that is the Eucharist. There we will find the strength to make a gift of ourselves to God and to each other. There we shall find the strength to wash one another's feet and to live the Great Commandment of love.

If we do not flee from the cross of pain and humiliation, if we stand firm in who we are and what we stand for, if we work together, hierarchy, priests, religious and laity, to live our faith and fulfill our mission, then we will be a stronger and holier church.

✝

Perform the Works of Mercy

1) Feed the hungry.
2) Give drink to the thirsty.
3) Clothe the naked.
4) Shelter the homeless.
5) Visit the sick.
6) Visit those in prison.
7) Bury the dead.
8) Help people understand and learn.
9) Counsel the doubtful.
10) Convert the sinner.
11) Comfort the sorrowful.
12) Forgive injuries.
13) Bear wrongs patiently.
14) Pray for the living and the dead.

✝

Follow The Ten Commandments

1. I am the Lord thy God. Thou shall not have strange gods before me.
2. Thou shall not take the name of the Lord thy God in vain.
3. Remember thou keep the Sabbath Day.
4. Honor thy Father and thy Mother.
5. Thou shall not kill.
6. Thou shall not commit adultery.
7. Thou shall not steal.
8. Thou shall not bear false witness against thy neighbor.
9. Thou shall not covet thy neighbor's wife.
10. Thou shall not covet thy neighbor's goods.

✝

Defend The Faith

The world needs to hear the voice of the Catholic Church. We are that voice. We are the boys and girls and men and women who comprise 98% of the Catholic Church, the laity. In every city and town, in every coffee shop and boardroom, on every radio and television station, in every newspaper and magazine, through the Internet and electronic mail, hear us. We are Catholics. We are one billion strong and we proclaim a joyous, life-affirming moral message. We believe in Jesus Christ.

This is a call to action. We must be activists in defense of our faith. We can't roll over in bed on Sunday. We can't turn a deaf ear to those who casually malign our beliefs. We can't daydream while the political, economic and cultural agendas are crafted and imposed by others. The complacent and the apathetic are the weakest among us. The strongest among us must get up and speak up.

We can influence the world through our prayers, our words and our example. We are positive. We are hopeful. We are Catholics. We are one billion strong and we proclaim a joyous, life-affirming moral message. We believe in Jesus Christ.

✝

Pray The Rosary

For over 500 years, the Rosary has served as a visible Catholic symbol of devotion in honor of the Virgin Mary. The word *"Rosary"* comes from the Latin meaning a *"crown or garland of roses."* Each Hail Mary symbolizes the gift of a rose to our Lady. While saying the Rosary, we join with Mary in our prayers to the Father. Mother Mary has promised us, *"You shall obtain all you ask of me by the recitation of the Rosary."*

The Rosary engages us in blessed prayer both vocal, saying Our Fathers and Hail Marys, and mental, reflecting on the mysteries of the life of Christ and His Mother. The Rosary is divided into five decades representing an event in Christ's life. There are four sets of *"Mysteries of the Rosary:"* Joyful, Luminous, Sorrowful and Glorious.

As Pope John Paul II has reminded us, *"We need to return to the practice of family prayer and prayer for families."* The Rosary presents a wonderful opportunity to follow the Pope's guidance.

To learn more about the benefits of reciting the Rosary, you may wish to visit: www.rosary-center.org; www.virtualrosary.org; www.theholyrosary.org.

✝

Teach the Faith

How will the younger generation of Catholics learn about their faith? How will we be able to influence the national debate on life, peace and cultural issues? How will we be able to answer and reason with the cynics, critics and those with justifiable concerns? We must study, practice and teach our Catholic faith. Knowledge is power. As parishioners, as parents, as individuals, we must make a life long commitment to broaden and share our Catholic educations.

There is a wonderful interesting history to our faith. There is excitement and inspiration to be found in the lives of the saints. There is a deep satisfaction from the bonds we share with our priests and sisters and brothers who have served so many millions in so many places so selflessly. This is our Catholic tradition. This is our Catholic heritage; over two thousand years of service in the name of God.

Read the Bible and other books on Catholic doctrine. Study the catechism. Subscribe to Catholic magazines and newspapers. Visit Catholic websites. Watch Catholic television. Know where we have been. Know where we are now. Know where we are going, stronger and wiser.

✝

Converse With Your Friend

Give me persons of prayer and they will be capable of anything. St. Vincent De Paul

God is your friend and your prayers are your conversation with your friend. Like any good friend, God wants to hear about your hopes and dreams and troubles and concerns. Like any good friend, God comforts and strengthens you. He shares his wisdom, grace and love with you. His Holy Spirit fills you with hope and enthusiasm.

Don't get overly concerned with the mechanics or rituals of prayer. As Pope John Paul II teaches, *"Pray any way you like, so long as you do pray."* Use a prayer book or rosary beads or just open your heart to a friend. Speak with devotion and humility and confidence. Every time you see a sunset or hear a child's laugh or receive a wish and you thank God, you are praying. Every time you work hard or help another and you offer your efforts in God's name, you are praying. As Jesus Christ has promised us, *"Ask and it shall be given to you."* Wow, what a friend!

✝

Celebrate The Sacraments

Baptism
Eucharist
Reconciliation
Confirmation
Marriage
Holy Orders
Anointing of the Sick

✝

Claim the Fruits of the Holy Spirit

1. Charity

2. Joy

3. Peace

4. Patience

5. Benignity

6. Goodness

7. Long-suffering

8. Mildness

9. Faith

10. Modesty

11. Continence

12. Chastity

✝

Remember
The Beatitudes

- Blessed are the poor in spirit: for theirs is the kingdom of heaven.

- Blessed are the meek: for they shall possess the land.

- Blessed are they who mourn: for they shall be comforted.

- Blessed are they that hunger and thirst after justice: for they shall have their fill.

- Blessed are the merciful: for they shall obtain mercy.

- Blessed are the clean of heart: for they shall see God.

- Blessed are the peacemakers: for they shall be called the children of God.

- Blessed are they that suffer persecution for justice' sake, for theirs is the kingdom of heaven.

1

Set Goals

Unless you shape your life, circumstances will shape it for you. You have to work, sacrifice, invest, and persist to get the results you want. Choose them well. You can't start your planning until you know where you want to go.

God has given you the free will to choose your life's direction. Have others already done what you want to do? Study them and do what they did. Start anywhere, at anytime, and persist. Stop worrying what others think about what you can or can't do. Believe in yourself and your abilities. Have the self-confidence to challenge your current situation. This is your life to live; it's day by day and step by step.

Write down your goals. Only three percent of people have written goals and only one percent review those written goals daily. Be in that elite one percent. Visualize the attainment of your goals often. Goals are dreams with dates attached. You will only become as great and as happy as the goals you choose.

2

Divide and Conquer

A common denominator among the successful is that they are focused on the immediate accomplishment of specific objectives. Separate the important from the urgent and allow time for both. Break down any large task into a series of small tasks and start taking action. In the beginning, don't be too concerned with how you will achieve your goals. With commitment, research and patience, the means will come. Answers materialize when the facts have been collected. Your goals will evolve into a set of action-oriented objectives, which will become a series of to-dos.

Now prioritize. If you don't prioritize your day's activities, everything is of equal importance. Whether one thing gets done or not doesn't matter. You want your activities to be important, to have had a clearly defined purpose. Write your to-do list every day. Prioritize it. Make at least one of your daily objectives a challenge. At the end of each day, you'll be able to relax and bask in that wonderful feeling of accomplishment.

3

Write a Personal Mission Statement

Create for yourself an evolving document that outlines your purpose in life. Who are you? What are your values? What do you intend to do with your time to make your one life meaningful? Because God has blessed you with the gift of free will, you can determine your own future. You don't have to listen to those who say you are too old, too young, too poor, too unattractive, too uneducated or the wrong color, gender or nationality. They are not speaking of someone following the Action Principles® guided by the Catholic faith.

When you read inspirational passages in the Bible, books, magazines or newspapers, copy them. When you hear inspirational passages in homilies, write them down. Put everything together in a folder or box. This will serve as your motivational reserve and will help you create a personal mission statement.

Your mission statement only has to be a few sentences or paragraphs. Refer to your mission statement periodically and don't be afraid to change it as you grow. A mission statement will help you to establish a foundation upon which you can build your dreams and goals and from which will flow your objectives and daily to-do list.

4

Follow Through

Follow through to make sure that you've done the job right. Follow through to say thank you and offer new ideas. Follow through to ask for more business. You earn respect by saying what you're prepared to do and then doing exactly that. Follow through shows that you are a person of your word and someone who cares. It shows that you are accessible and that you want to keep the lines of communication open. You may make mistakes and follow through gives you the opportunity to correct and to learn from those mistakes. Personalize your follow-up with handwritten notes and phone calls. Small gifts, tickets and lunches may also be appropriate follow-up incentives. Check up on yourself and reap the rewards. Follow through amplifies your effectiveness.

5

Submit to a Higher Power

Look at the big picture. You build your life upon your Catholic faith. You cherish your Catholic faith. You aren't afraid to tell others of your beliefs. You stand for positive values. You are ethical in your dealings. You pray and meditate to have the courage to face your fears. You pray and meditate to have the strength to accept, endure and triumph over the hardships and small daily annoyances that the path to success will present. You celebrate the good that you find in the world.

With humility, submit. You are but one fragile, fallible human. Every religion has prayers. A prayer is your conversation with God. Your success and happiness is God's answer. Your selfless good works in helping others are your prayers put into action.

6

Don't Complicate Matters

Don't complicate your life. Think before you act. Look for the simple ways or answers first where less can go wrong. Work from your basics. Make sure that you understand the assignment or the problem before you begin. What are the time and performance expectations that will indicate satisfactory completion? Reexamine how you are doing things. Is a task consuming all of your time? Is it worth the time you are investing? Do you have the necessary resources? Can it be delegated? If so, is the right person assigned to complete the job? Your research, your quiet time, your commitment to teamwork and your prioritized to-do list should all help. Pare away the unnecessary. Even the philosophy underlying these Catholic Action Principles™ can be stated very simply. Improve yourself and help others.

7

Commit to Never Ending Improvement

Constantly seek ways to do things better in all areas of your life. The Japanese have a word for the concept of never ending improvement, "*kaizen*." Progress and ultimate success come to those who train and keep training. If you choose to stop and become aware, you can become a better spouse, son, daughter, friend, employer, employee, athlete, citizen and servant of God.

Commitment comes from the inside out and is tested often. Measure yourself against the best. Most others will choose to be average. This is what average means. You won't know your limits if you don't keep trying. Reject the idea of good enough. Commit to excellence. Take each of your goals and think of how you can improve one percent each month. Success is a journey. It is not a quick fix. The joy is in the doing. Think of success not as a peak to be climbed but a high plateau to be walked.

Always encourage children or employees to do their best and to keep going. Set the bar high for yourself and them. You will all be the better for it.

8

Be Frugal

Separate your wants from your needs. You want to work for all you need, not necessarily for all you want. You do not have to sentence yourself to a lifetime of hard labor for the false trappings of status. Living on less can eventually yield much more. The simpler you make your life, the easier it will be to maintain. Think in terms of moderation. It is easier to buy things than to sell them. You can make a comfortable life for yourself by finding contentment in the things you already have and holding reasonable expectations. Look to the saints as examples.

Be pragmatic. To build an investment bankroll, you can work more or you can spend less. Many people who write and stick to a household budget find that the simple act of thinking and organizing before spending can yield savings of between 10% - 15% of their earnings without seriously compromising their lifestyles. Give yourself a raise by being frugal.

9

Make Today Special

This is the day which the Lord has given; let us rejoice. Many people enjoy using the first few minutes of the day for their reflective time. How did yesterday go? What do you want to accomplish today? What will be most important? This, of course, becomes your prioritized to-do list. How will today vary from your usual routine? Can you think of any small things that you can do? Perhaps there is something that you've been avoiding, that, if you do it, would make you feel especially proud of yourself.

Give each day a specific purpose. For unsuccessful, unhappy people, there is often a sameness to their days. Is it Monday or Thursday? Is it March or November? Is it 3 o'clock in the afternoon or 10 o'clock in the morning? They're in a rut and it doesn't matter.

Everybody has the same amount of time each day. How are you going to spend your 24 hours? Plan in advance. Make lists. Lists are your road map to personal accomplishment and balanced living. Always carry paper and pen. What are you doing today to ensure a better tomorrow for yourself and your family?

In Loving Memory of John [Jay] LaBossiere

10

Record Your Thoughts

Carry index cards, a hand-held computer or a small notebook. Borrow napkins to write on. As you become an action-oriented person, positive thoughts will occur with increasing regularity. Write down your ideas. You will have good ideas because you will have many ideas. Review your notes before your quiet time or before bed. You will become your own best thera-  pist. You will see the ways to solve your own prob- lems, find your own route to hap- piness and realize your own dreams. Spend most of your time thinking about solutions and not problems. Get back to recording your thoughts.

11

Use the Power of Patience

You can handle most problems because you know that only a little time stands between you and your goal. It may take twenty calls to make a sale. Be patient. It might take you five attempts to quit smoking or lose weight. It might take ten applications to get the job you really want. The point is that you try and keep trying until you succeed. Most people quit too soon. Be persistent. Be patient. Concentrate on your major goal until you have achieved it. It is not what you did yesterday. It is not what you may be doing today. It is what you are prepared to do every day. That one cold morning when you want to roll over but instead get up and go to the gym, is a defining moment.

Remember that all wealth, all businesses, all real estate and all treasures eventually pass from old hands to young. Be prepared. Your time is coming.

12

Maintain A Positive Mental Attitude

A positive mental attitude results from a life guided by faith and dedicated to self-improvement and service. With a personal commitment to doing your best today, you don't have to be overly concerned about tomorrow. You can be confident that good things will happen and be equally confident that if trouble comes you will have the strength of your Catholic religion to cope. You are tough. You stay at it. You don't allow your doubts to destroy your dreams. Hope does spring eternal.

You are thankful to have the curiosity to keep learning. You are grateful to see opportunity knock so often. You are thankful to have the personality to keep making new friends. Your mind can only hold one thought at a time so make that one thought positive. Count your blessings. Say your prayers. The way is clear. The world is a better place because you are in it.

13

Risk Failure

Be ready. There is no better time to start taking positive action than right now. You research and you have confidence in your preparations. You don't allow yourself to become paralyzed by indecision. You realize that a time comes when you must act. If you hesitate too long, doubts will linger and turn into fears. Yes, you may stumble. Yes, you may be rejected. Yes, you may fail. This is life, but your Catholic faith gives you hope, support and the heart to try again. You will find guidance from your prayers. Life's winners accept that in trying they may have to adjust and even start again and again. The difference between successful people and others is not whether you make mistakes or even temporarily fail, but how you respond.

Many people look for guarantees before taking independent action. Yet, in seeking assurances, they frequently receive cautions, which can easily be used as excuses for inaction. Be aware that those who love you the most may be the loudest in warning you not to risk.

14

Get Tough

Tough means that you are willing to stand tall and persevere. Even when your mind and body signal perfectly good reasons for giving up, you go on. This tough is obvious. But tough can be seen every day if we choose to look. Tough may be a patient undergoing cancer treatments or a single mother struggling to raise children. Tough can be an alcoholic ready to face rehab or an athlete living in a wheelchair. Tough can be rejecting false praise and honestly accepting you and your children for who and what you are. Tough can be standing up to cynics, skeptics and comics who mock your faith. Tough is an ability to make the best from what you are given. Tough is making the decision to replace self-pity, complaints and dependence with self-reliance, independence and action.

You've got to be tough to do the big things in life like taking risks, admitting mistakes, and changing bad habits. You've got to be tough to do the little things like biting your tongue, waiting your turn and putting up with fools. Self-reliance and self-confidence will demand your toughness. Then, you must temper toughness with kindness, realizing that many times it will be tough to be kind. Be kind anyway.

15

Cause Change

The status quo may be comforting, but for there to be growth, there must be change. Since you seek growth, you must seek change. You must see yourself and your environment not only as it is, but also as it could and should be. You seek the changes necessary to reach the better you so that you can play your part in making a better world.

First, you change yourself. Can you change your day and spend more time with your family? Can you change your standard lunch routine and make a visit to Church? Can you change your drive home and stop at a nursing home for twenty minutes and see someone who may have few visitors? Can you change your office habits and find the time to make five more phone calls? What are the possible consequences of not changing? Realize that many people don't make plans because they don't want to risk any change. Doing little with your life is much easier and safer than taking risks, but then you will be a small person. Instead, seek the changes which will allow you to be all that you can be.

16

Pass the Test

Life is a test and the points on that test are earned by how much attention you give to improving yourself and helping others. When your test is graded by God, to what will you attribute your success: study, hard work, personality, talent, skill, opportunity, connections, patronage or luck? No amount of material success earned and kept will be awarded credit. The greater your blessings, the greater your obligation to share your good fortune.

Use your special talents to serve the common good. Let your actions be motivated by a commitment to charity and justice. Be compassionate, kind and considerate. Free yourself from your attachment to things. Think of the example of Saint Francis. Right now is the time to consider your blessings. Start scoring points. Live the life of a good Catholic today and every day. Heaven awaits.

17

Accept Differences

See each person as an individual and not as part of a group. All humans from all countries and cultures are equal without regard to race, color, creed or gender. Believe with confidence and trust that the vast majority of people whom you meet, befriend or do business with are more similar than different from you.

People are inherently good. Most people act in good faith. Most people believe in God. They mean you no harm and would assist you in time of need. Don't waste your time thinking otherwise. Do not become a party to rumor or gossip.

Reject stereotypes and the divisive and demeaning policies that group people into categories. Be the first to build bridges of tolerance and understanding.

18

Master Success

There is a master of goodness and faith inside you. It is an ideal. It is you at your best. Keep working.

You are calm, thoughtful, patient and confident.

You are honest, trustworthy, responsible and reliable.

You are loyal and proud.

You are humble and reverent.

You are tough, self-reliant, persistent and hard working.

You are organized, neat and poised.

You are inquisitive and teachable.

You are healthy, vibrant and enthusiastic.

You are kind, friendly, helpful and generous.

You are brave and daring.

You are moral and ethical.

You are a good Catholic.

19

Spread Your Enthusiasm

Living your Catholic faith and putting the Catholic Action Principles™ to work in your life will elevate your soul and lift your spirit. You will feel a zest for life. You will live full, enriched days. This will happen because you will have taken the quiet time to think, organize and prioritize your days. You will love many things and these things will become part of your day. You will be in control. Every day you will do good things for yourself and others. Words like boring, bland and uneventful will rarely describe your work or your relationships.

Listen to your favorite CD. Call a friend. Say a rosary. Read a good book. Smile. Hear. See. Feel. Smell. Take a walk and look at all the God given wonders of your world. Let everyone in your life know that, as Bishop Sheen taught us, *life is worth living.*

Be known as a motivator. Ask others about their goals and how you can help them. Make people feel part of a successful team. Solicit their input. Keep everyone informed and involved. Establish performance incentives. Look for opportunities to praise and reward. Enthusiasm is contagious.

20

Applaud the Beginner

You walk into a karate school for a first visit and see kicking, punching, blocking, chopping and flipping. It can be intimidating if you've never done these things. Or, you may look and feel awkward learning to snow ski or rollerblade or taking a foreign language. But persist; this is your first day and there will never be another first day.

Any new endeavor may be tough in the beginning. Accept this. You must believe in yourself. Initially, critics may feel free to ridicule your ideas and goals as foolish and unrealistic. When you ultimately succeed, everyone will claim to have been on your team from the beginning. Take action and persist. Applaud those who try, because the first step is often the toughest. Welcome the newcomer.

21

Give Yourself the Gift of Self-Reliance

Combined with your Catholic faith, if there is one other gift that you can give yourself that will enhance the overall quality of your life, it is self-reliance. You already possess everything you will need to succeed. You can work on your own schedule toward your own goals without feeling pressured by the demands of others.

When you are self-reliant, if you lose your job, you'll get another. If you lose that job, you'll start your own business. You can make more money as a self-employed handyman applying the Action Principles® to your work than a lazy lawyer will ever earn. You need the will, the self-confidence and a realistic plan. As a follower of the Catholic faith, you will have them. Life just can't get you down because you are in control of yourself.

22

Lead by Example

Start acting immediately as the person you will be, a person of character with a sound reputation, a better Catholic. Your words, your manner, your attitude, your dress, your posture and your actions are all reflections. In modern society, people are constantly bombarded with visual and auditory messages. People need cues to sort good from bad and to find order so that they can make decisions. In many different aspects of your daily life, you are giving off cues that can be positive or negative. If you speak well, dress appropriately, smile, are courteous, work hard, volunteer and don't complain, in short, acting religiously, you give people the chance to view you in your best light.

You must never expect others to do what you would not do. You must be fair, firm, friendly and dependable. If you have to correct someone, do it in private. You have succeeded as a leader when your team works just as well in your absence. Be constantly on the lookout for heroes in your own life to admire and emulate. Adopt their styles. Then, lead by example.

23

Control Conflict

Remain calm and detached. Pause and say a *"Hail Mary."* Allow others to rage while you consider the appropriate response. Should you reason, agree, apologize, fight or leave? Which is to your benefit and to the benefit of those you must protect? Arguing often makes the other party become more defensive and determined to prevail. Let go of your anger. It only clouds the issue and draws you into a quick response. Whenever possible use kindness as your weapon against evil. Neutralize shouting with soft words. Answer threats with serene confidence. Speak plainly. Don't use foul language or sarcasm. Breathe deeply with long exhalations. Let the anger wash over you. Maintain your presence. Don't exaggerate. Don't lie. Attack the argument and not the person.

Long-term relationships are almost always more important than short-term problems. Be an active peacemaker, building bridges of understanding.

24

Listen to Your Instincts

"I don't feel comfortable here. I don't like the sound of this. This doesn't look right to me."

With regard to your body or surroundings, your instincts are your best early warning system. Listen to the inner voice. Listen to that gut feeling. Go to the doctor. Leave the party. Get away from these people. Quit this job. Don't open that door. Duck into that store. The world is an imperfect place. There are dangerous places and people. There are angels and there are demons.

Every once in a while, your instincts may be off and you may feel foolish. Err on the side of safety and your instincts may save you from danger. Give yourself time or space to consider your options. It is foolhardy to do otherwise.

25

Face Fear

Knowledge, practice, courage and faith are your weapons against fear.

One person can step out of an airplane door at 2,000 feet without hesitation. Another can stand before an audience of 2,000 and give a speech without breaking into a sweat. Fears can be rational or irrational, but they are always personal and real. Everyone fears something.

To diminish a fear, you must first face it. The one hundredth skydive or speech won't be as traumatic as the first. The best way to deal with first fears is through a combination of logic and bravery. Logically, most people who jump from planes or give speeches don't die. They succeed through preparation. If your equipment is right and your training is complete, you are ready to jump. If your speech is carefully crafted and practiced, you are ready to speak. Why do many people pray in fearful times? Because it works.

Associate with confident people. You have seen many who have already done what you fear doing. Now, do what they have done. Courage grows with action. Fear is learned and must be unlearned. After facing that fear, you will feel exhilarated. Without fear, there can be no courage. Fear provides the opportunity to be brave.

26

Don't Be A Perfectionist

Two things you should know about God. One, there is a God. Two, you are not God. Trying to be perfect takes too much time and effort. It creates too much stress and is impossible anyway. Instead, strive to relax at the 90% level. This is the personal mastery level. Following the Catholic Action Principles™ and living the Catholic faith, reaching the 90% level in most of your financial and social endeavors will be something that you don't even have to think about. It will happen through your persistence, determination, hard work and nice personality.

Right now, learn about the income and the lifestyle level of those in the top 10% of your profession. If you aren't content earning more than 90% of your co-workers, choose another profession.

It is possible to try too hard in business, exercise and relationships. Overwork can produce stress and anxiety, which is the opposite of the inner peace you seek. Your best is good enough. Live to a high standard, not to an impossible obsession.

27

Remain Adaptable

In daily life, through a love of many things, it is possible to remain adaptable. If it starts raining on the way to the beach, you'll enjoy going to the movies. If you are kept waiting for an appointment, don't get angry. Say a decade of the Rosary, make a few calls or work on your schedule. If you get stuck in traffic, enjoy your favorite motivational audiotape, radio station or CD. Always have a book with you and you will never be alone. The small stuff can't get you down if you are ready to substitute one good thing for another.

28

Think
Win–Win

Thinking win-win is a frame of mind that seeks mutual benefit and is based on mutual respect. It is about bargaining fairly, and being open-minded and reasonable to all parties. It is acting Catholic. It is about compromise and a sincere desire to find agreements that occupy the middle ground. Win-win is not taking advantage when it is understood that you are being trusted to act with honor.

It's about thinking in terms of abundance. There is an ever-expanding *"pie,"* a cornucopia of opportunity, wealth, and resources, not scarcity and adversarial competition.

29

Be Proud

Take pride in who you are and in those values and beliefs for which you stand. Be proud of your Catholic faith. Be proud of your education, work and personal accomplishments. Be proud of your spouse, children and extended family. Be proud of your home and neighborhood. Be proud of your country. Be proud of your body, personal grooming and your manners. Be proud of the sports teams and cultural organizations that you support. Be proud of your government officials when they stand selflessly for the public good.

Don't be afraid of who you are, since you act with courage and compassion. Tell others, and bask in the feeling of being your best. Teach others, so they too may be proud, as we all try to be better Catholics.

30
Start It Now

You don't have to wait for permission to do the right thing. Be decisive. Take the initiative. Get the facts. Do it now. If you don't have time to send a letter to a sick friend, send a card, a fax or an e-mail. If you can't visit your mother, call her. If you see a gift that a friend would love, buy it for him or her. If you can't go to church for sixty minutes, go for forty minutes.

Avoid not doing things because you can't get them done exactly as you'd originally planned. Be bold and get in the habit of doing something. Walk down one block. Pay three bills. Spend fifteen minutes with your children's homework. Give five dollars to charity. Say grace before dinner. Small efforts done continually can yield significant, positive results. Do it now while it's on your mind. You don't have to be perfect to live the Catholic Action Principles™. Just be a person of action. You must have more than good intentions to succeed. Be good by doing good. You must act. Get it done. Start it now.

31

Be the Good Warrior

The warrior is tough in loyalty, intensity, determination, bearing, initiative, endurance, courage and strength of will. The warrior is soft in calmness, self-confidence and compassion. The warrior is frequently called upon to step forward when most gladly step back. Warriors exist on the battlefield and in daily life.

People may react to you rudely, selfishly and with malice. Be courteous anyway.

Those you help may whine and offer no thanks. Help them anyway.

Your honest words may be challenged and ridiculed. Speak anyway.

Success may involve many mistakes and disappointments. Try anyway.

Your donations may seem too small to matter. Give anyway.

A warrior can be a good Catholic.

32

Embody Integrity

As a follower of the Catholic Action Principles™, you are proud, strong, friendly, generous and successful. As a good Catholic, many will seek your counsel. People will depend on you. Have faith and a belief in your cause. Know what you will fight for and what you won't. Do not compromise what is right. Stick to your convictions and principles as you allow your ethical values to direct your decision-making. Integrity goes beyond self-interest to moral courage. Lying only leads to more lying.

Keep your promises. Fulfill your commitments. People want to know where you stand and for what you stand. People respect honesty and sincerity, but hate hypocrisy. Be consistent. Speak in clear precise facts. Be sure your words match your deeds. Do what you say and your credibility builds. You cannot speak stronger words than, *"I am a Catholic and I give you my word."*

33

Stay Centered

In the battles of life, you will take punches. Some may hurt. This too will pass. You are the center of your universe. Take care of your own needs first. Then go to your family, then to friends, neighbors and employees. Move on to the larger communities. Don't use saving the world as an excuse to forget your family. Don't allow others to rush or pressure you to act before you can decide what is right. The most important thing that a father can do for his children is to love their mother. The most important thing that parents can do for their children is to raise them in the Catholic faith.

Stand with your knees slightly bent. Head up. Breathe deeply from your belly. You are a very small part of the grand scheme of things. You are one with the universe. You are everything and nothing. Remain calm, balanced and aware. In a moment, a short prayer can bring you back to center.

In Loving Memory of Robert and Margaret McElearney

34

Love Many Things

You proportionally increase your chances for happiness by increasing the number of things that you love doing. Love many things and your happiness will escalate into an enthusiasm for life, which will have a positive effect on you and those around you. Seek and enjoy those things that give your life value and purpose.

To love many things, you must be adventurous. A boring life is your own fault. Try new things. Be excited and passionate about life. Feel good. You must be able to see beauty in the grand scheme of things as well as in details.

Discover: music, art, books, food, T'ai Chi, theater, travel, movies, sunsets, exercise, friends, gardens, religious retreats and the Internet. Open your mind. Find your preferences. Make your home and office beautiful places to love. Keep going …

Remember how lucky you are to have so many interests. Happiness may not be a result of financial success. Happiness is a result of loving many things and appreciating what you already have. God has given you much to love.

35

Forget Everybody

Not everybody wants to do business with you. Not everybody wants to be your friend. Not everybody wants world peace. Not everybody wants to work hard. Not everybody wants to be president.

Not everybody is smart enough to be a rocket scientist. Not everybody is fast enough to run in the Olympics. Who is helped by pretending otherwise?

Trying to accommodate everybody is a trap. It can't be done. Be yourself. People know their own problems better than you do. Not everybody will listen to reason or even act in his or her own best interest. You can. Guided by your Catholic faith and supported by your prayers, you will know the positive actions you are called to make.

36

Maintain Your Presence

Your contented presence shows an air of simple elegance and refinement in attitude and form. You appear physically, emotionally and spiritually strong, yet you seem to have even greater strength in reserve. You are poised, coordinated and balanced. You command with effortless, assured confidence. Be calm. Be deliberate. Feel assured and alert. Look good. Feel good. Keep your head up and your shoulders back. Keep your eyes forward. Breathe deeply. Speak with a soft voice in a thoughtful manner. Rarely interrupt. Be brief. Walk with a purpose. Don't rush. Have a firm handshake. Your eyes are friendly. Your demeanor is respectful. Let your smile begin in your mind. You exhibit both style and class. First impressions are lasting.

The things you want drawn to you will come as a result of your good nature and determined persistence. Pause and savor the moment. Begin your work. You are a practicing Catholic.

37

Act As You Feel

When you feel in the mood to do something, this is the best time to do it.

If you feel happy, smile.

If you feel daring, act.

If you receive good service, compliment.

If you feel energetic, do something positive.

If you know a good joke, tell it.

If you feel generous, give.

If you are interested in becoming wealthy, save and invest.

If someone needs help, lend them your strong hands or soft voice.

If you give your word, keep it.

If you want to make things better, vote.

In Loving Memory of Paul Carr

38

Appreciate Your Appeal

Being a practicing Catholic makes you an appealing, charismatic person. Students will want to learn from you, bosses to promote you and customers to buy your products or services.

Your allure will be your genuine selflessness in wanting to help them to achieve their objective, whether it is to become a black belt or buy a car. By not trying to be a preacher but rather to set a good example, your influence will inspire as it expands. Charisma isn't painted on the outside. It comes from the inside. Be honest. Be yourself. Adopt this attitude and you will be liked by many – immediately.

39

Develop Your Sense of Humor

In all areas of life, a quick wit, a hearty laugh, a smile and a warm sense of humor are appreciated. To be a good joke teller, tell jokes often. Practice. Model your delivery after comedians you admire and funny friends. Start a joke file.

Always be absolutely sure that your material is clean and non-offensive. Stick to a universally funny subject – you. Most of the best humor is self-deprecating. That is, you have to learn to laugh at yourself. On your road to success, there will be many stumbles and fumbles, providing many opportunities for you to turn the unexpected into stress-reducing laughter. Don't sweat the small stuff. Laugh about it. Be affable. Humor will add to your attractiveness.

40

Become Grateful

Life isn't exactly the way you want it to be. You will have your ups and downs and crosses to bear. You will have opportunities to practice holding your tongue and exercising patience. Yet, because you are guided by your Catholic faith, you will be able to keep everyday events in perspective.

Be grateful for all you have. Acknowledge and accept compliments. In the larger scheme of things, you may wish to be grateful for good health, a supportive spouse, a rewarding profession, obedient, healthy children, conscientious employees, prosperity, loyal friends and even winning sports teams. You add and choose. Why not write letters to people in your life who have made a difference and thank them? You will both feel good.

When you embrace gratitude, you can help others do the same. Hold the burning candle from which others can light their candles.

41

Show Loyalty

Be a stand-up person. You stand for your family, country, friends and Catholic faith. When and if trouble comes, let others have no doubt that they can count on you for help and support. Your commitments don't waver with the moods of the moment. You don't hesitate to act.

You are consistent, devoted, faithful and true. You aren't a one-day-a-week Catholic. You are a Catholic through and through. You stand for your beliefs and values. You aren't afraid to pledge allegiance to what is right. You will speak and act for the unborn, the homeless, the lonely, the condemned, the underrepresented and the mistreated. You will speak and act for world peace. You will speak and act in support of our clergy. This is loyalty.

42
Let It Go

Anger, hatred, bitterness, resentments and thoughts of revenge are heavy weights that slow a person down. Allowed to fester, these negative feelings can consume increasingly larger portions of your life. Liberate yourself. Let it go. The forgiving person is always stronger. Be like the rock in the stream and let the thoughts of revenge flow by you.

As a good Catholic, as a person of action, you will continue to make lots of mistakes. You will do foolish things. Learn the lesson. You can ask man and pray to God for forgiveness.

Can you say, *"I'm sorry and I apologize if I offended you."*? Can you say, *"Forgive them Father for they know not what they are doing."*? Lighten your burden. Continue to encourage efforts at reconciliation.

43

Demonstrate Your Love

From the Bible, we learn that love is patient and kind. It does not envy. It does not boast. It is not proud. It is not rude; it is not self-seeking; it is not easily angered; it keeps no record of wrongs. It always protects, always trusts, always hopes, always perseveres. It is responsibility and a willingness to work out problems.

Love is too wonderful and too powerful to be kept bottled up. Let it out with your smiles, your voice, your manner, your enthusiasm and your continuing acts of kindness. For love, you can risk being vulnerable.

When you find love, cherish and safeguard it. A loving marriage and family is worth all your efforts.

44

Be Prudent

Just because you deserve victory doesn't mean that you will win every fight, game or argument. Someone else may have the tactical advantage. Have the self-confidence to know when not to fight. Perhaps the smartest course of action is to retreat and reflect upon your options. Can the matter be settled in a non-confrontational, non-aggressive way? Will you turn the other cheek? How far are you willing to go to preserve peace?

The non-action of the wise man is not inaction. It is not studied. It is not shaken by anything. The heart of the wise man is tranquil. It is the mirror of heaven and earth ... emptiness, stillness and tranquility. Wise men don't fight each other.

45

Develop Your Special Talent

You were born with a God-given special talent. It may be to sing, write, teach, paint, mentor, preach, defend or befriend. You have something special to offer the world, something you can do better than 10,000 others. You must keep learning and trying new things to find your special talent. The world needs your gift. Be aware that even a special talent can go stale if you don't keep using and honing it. Endeavor to keep your talents and all your skills up to date.

An advantage isn't an advantage unless you use it. Find ways to use your advantages to set and reach your goals. Likewise, you should recognize and then try to minimize the impact of your limitations. Remember that not all advantages are transferable. Just because you are talented in one area doesn't mean that you will be talented at everything you try. The successful real estate investor can easily lose her money opening a restaurant. Stick to your advantages and don't stray from them without reasoned justification.

46

Be Persistent

Modern life can make you soft. The status quo may become comfortably familiar. You can actually begin to believe that you are doing all that you can, or that doing more isn't worth the effort. Challenge yourself. You must start the positive momentum in your life and then you've got to stick with it day to day.

You don't need someone else to tell you not to smoke. If today, you smoked a pack, tomorrow smoke 18. The next day, 17. Improve. If you haven't read a book recently, read one. If you don't exercise, take a walk around the block. If you're shy, say to five new people: *"Good morning!"*

You know yourself. You know what improvement you need. You don't need anyone to tell you not to jump from a fifty-story building, so why would you need someone to tell you not to do drugs, to exercise more, eat a sensible diet, talk to your kids, go to Church, say your prayers or compliment your employees? You know what to do.

Keep going. No one can say that you failed until you do. Keep taking small steps toward your goal. Challenge the you who is content with yesterday's accomplishments. Take a deep breath. Changes that last a lifetime begin in a moment. With persistence, only time stands between you and your goal.

47

Develop Winning Habits

If becoming a success were easy, everyone would do it. It isn't. They don't. As a follower of the Catholic Action Principles™, you can. You can develop winning habits while identifying and working to eliminate your bad habits. Be patient. Psychological studies have shown that it takes about 30 days to begin to form or begin to rid yourself of a habit.

You can keep your word even though this may not always be easy. You can write and focus on your goals and objectives and your to-do list. You can exercise when you're tired. You can get the whole family to Mass on Sundays and Holy Days. You can volunteer. You can give a little extra money to charity. You can give a little extra time to family members, students and customers. You can pick up litter on the jogging path. You can delay gratification. You can do a lot while others are idle.

You won't always want to do these things. You will feel that you are doing more than your share. You are right. Work on your habits. You are tough.

48

Do What Others Can't

Most people can't give two nights a month to volunteer at a hospice. You can.

Most people can't get up at 6:00 AM and jog two miles. You can.

Most people can't give up their lunch hour to solve a customer's problem. You can.

Most people can't help to clean up other people's messes. You can.

Most people can't help a friend deal with destructive behavior. You can.

Most people can't give five percent of their money to charity. You can.

You are a practicing Catholic.

49

Accept Hard Work

Great accomplishments come from hard work. Luck accompanies hard work. If necessary, be prepared to endure temporary hardship. At times, the work is going to be hard to do and you would prefer doing something easier. Accept this. Put enthusiasm into your work and you will reduce boredom. Commit yourself to hard work and be thankful that you aren't lazy. Laziness makes all work difficult.

From day one, you accept the premise that by following the Catholic faith, you will work hard and give much. Don't cheat, or look for the easy way out. Bask in the feeling of exhilaration and accomplishment that few will experience. In the end, you will discover that all the hard work was worth it. Work hard and don't wish that your life were any other way. Get accustomed to doing what others can't or won't.

50

Venture Outside the Box

It would be nice if there were logical step-by-step instructions for every step on your success journey. But, there aren't. You learn from your own experiences and by studying the experiences of others, and then you often have to find your own way. To find an answer, you may have to go outside the box.

If all graphic designers are offering computer-generated work, maybe your niche is hand drawing. If all your day care center competitors are strict about pick-up times, maybe your niche is to be flexible. If none of the other landlords in your area allow pets, maybe you do. Being a little different can be profitable.

If you can't earn a degree full time, perhaps you can take evening or correspondence or on-line courses. If you are worried about starting a business, you can consider buying an existing business or a franchise. If you can't exercise because you have to baby-sit, how about taking the kids for a walk or run with you? Don't give up. At times, you may have to improvise and be creative. Quitting or not trying isn't an option.

51

Communicate with Ease

Can you talk your way out of most tough situations? Can you talk to one person about returning to the Church? Can you talk to the media and garner positive press for your parish? Can you talk to 500 people and win converts to your cause or position? Can you answer critics of the Church with thoughtful argument?

Being an effective communicator can take you a long way and is a skill worth developing. Be yourself. Believe in your own words. It doesn't matter if you are talking to one person or one thousand. If you want people to like what you say, persuade with modesty and build your audience up.

Listen to good communicators and model yourself after them. How do good interviewers ask questions? How do good public speakers work? How do good salespeople sell? To communicate well, you can't get stuck on transmit. Pause before you speak. You must listen and speak with purpose. Get to the point. Create interest with visual aids. Tell them what you are going to tell them. Tell them. Tell them what you told them. Sit down. Prepare thoroughly and then relax. You'll be in God's hands.

Don't let technology leave you behind. Learn to communicate via email and the Internet.

52

Avoid Negative People

You have one life to live. You want to be happy and to make your life meaningful. You haven't got time to waste with negative people. They will drain your energy. When they find a willing audience, they won't let it go. They may have justifiable concerns but too often get involved in minor matters. They blame and look for excuses. Even when blame can be justified, it serves no productive good. They are usually negative because they have ceded control of their happiness to others – the boss, the neighbors, the kids, the politicians, the police.

Be polite and encouraging to negative people. Suggest returning to Church. Suggest clerical counsel. Suggest good books. Suggest helping others. Always offer kind words. You can be compassionate, but still be strong enough to walk away. Everyone has problems, but not everyone allows those problems to rule them. You can offer a temporary safe haven without becoming a permanent home.

53

Stay Fit and Healthy

Be prepared to succeed. You can swim, run, or rollerblade. You can take a walk. Staying fit also helps to prevent injury and helps you deal with stress and fatigue.

If you want to be thinner, start putting out more calories than you take in and you will lose weight. Start now. If you want to be healthier, add more fruits and vegetables to your diet. Drink a lot of water. If you want a strong heart, do twenty minutes of vigorous calisthenics each day. If you want to look good and feel strong, work out with weights three times a week for thirty minutes. You don't need fancy gym equipment to be fit. You don't need a lot of time. You just need the will to start and persist.

54

Relax Your Body

In your personal dealings, remain loose and light. Eliminate stress. There is rarely need to be tense and hardheaded. Much can be accomplished through calm reason and a soft voice.

Most physical movements should be loose, light, fluid, agile and flexible, rather than tense, hard, rigid and stiff. Slow, deep breathing will calm anxieties, lower your heart rate and allow for concentration. Massages, steam baths, saunas and whirlpools also help the muscles to rest. Make sure you get your rejuvenating 6-8 hours of sleep per night.

If you feel stressed, count 1001, 1002, 1003 before you speak. At any time, start counting backwards from 100 as you breathe deeply. Let the air fill your belly as you inhale and exhale, more slowly and more fully with each breath. Quiet your muscles and relax.

55

Invest In Your Future

Today, investors sacrifice and spenders enjoy. Tomorrow, investors enjoy and spenders keep working. If you buy a house today, you may have to work two jobs to make the mortgage payments now but you may own the house without debt in twenty years. If you give up TV tonight, you can take an evening course and in six years earn a college degree. If you start training today, you may be sore tomorrow and a black belt in four years. Invest in yourself.

Most wealthy people save between 15% and 20% of their income. Invest in fields in which you have a specialized knowledge. If you sell cars, invest in the auto industry. If you are a real estate broker, buy income properties. Be sure to diversify your holdings by investing in a retirement plan and a no-load mutual fund. There is a time value to money, so the earlier you start investing the better. Invest in things that appreciate rather than spend on things that depreciate. Secure your own retirement.

56

Retire Early

If you didn't have to worry about earning a living, you could concentrate on your personal potential and being of service to others.

You don't have to be a millionaire to retire early. In fact, if you had savings of half that amount, invested prudently, you could retire and earn an annual income that exceeds the annual income of 75% of the people in the United States. Over half of the people in the United States have less than $10,000 saved for retirement and live from paycheck to paycheck. They have no definitive financial plans. You are different. You now have a financial goal: to retire early.

Consider this: After 20 years of saving 20% of your income, you may create the choice of not having to work for a living.

Consider this: As an alternative to saving 20%, can you earn 20% more if you work 10 hours a day rather than 8, or 6 days a week rather than 5?

57

Have Faith

Look around the train, the classroom or the office and you will probably see ordinary people who are going to live ordinary lives. There is nothing wrong with this choice. But you feel differently. You read this book and you feel empowered. You go to Success.org for more training. Your mind fills with ideas. You find mentors. You research. You dare. You persist. You make money. You save. You invest. You succeed. You put your free time and extra money to good use. Many around you could have done exactly the same thing. They didn't. You did. Why?

You can't easily answer all of life's questions. You must have faith. Thank God for making you extraordinary. Thank God for helping you see so many possibilities. Thank God for making you a person of action.

58

Follow Your Code of Honor

As a Catholic follower of the Action Principles®, you adhere to a strict code of honor regarding your personal behavior. Your honor and faith become your shield.

You do not need to prove your might at the expense of others.

You do not need diplomas, awards or the acclaim of others to know who you are.

You do not need an audience to do the right thing.

You do not need a lot of money or many physical possessions to be happy.

You do not need to stand first in line.

You do not need coaxing to fulfill your religious obligations.

You do not need lessons to act civilly.

You do not need prompting to help someone in need.

59

Enjoy Quiet Time

We all need quiet time in our day when we can just be with our own thoughts. This isn't daydreaming. The serenity of quiet time can be enjoyed in a variety of ways. It can be traditional meditation, or walking the Stations of the Cross, gardening, reading Scripture, making a pot of tea or taking a long, hot shower. You may wish to say the Rosary.

Each day, take twenty minutes to stop, reflect and enjoy being who you are. Think about the past, present, future or nothing in particular. Relax by yourself and you will feel renewed. Tranquillity will re-energize you. Without trying, you will be amazed at how your subconscious mind releases so many good ideas. As you reflect upon the true sense for your existence, you can better deal with hardships.

Just as the time you spend exercising strengthens the physical you, quiet reflection strengthens the spiritual you. Quiet time also gives you the opportunity to practice minding your own business. Take a deep breath and continue to breathe slowly and steadily. Look around. Use all your senses. You will find contentment in the solitude; just ask a monk.

60

Look in the Mirror

Look at yourself as your family, co-workers, customers, students and the general public may be seeing you. Endeavor to like and admire what you and they see.

Don't kid yourself and fall victim to self-deception. Success means nothing if you are a professional athlete on drugs. Success means nothing if you are a doctor who is abusive at home. Success means nothing if your sole aim is to make your own life easier. Success means nothing if you fail to fulfill your religious obligations.

You can't honestly judge others if you can't honestly judge yourself. You cannot build a stronger self if you rely upon what may be the self-serving false appraisal and expectations of others. Do yourself a favor and be honest with yourself. Are you doing all you can do? If you are not honest with yourself, doubts and fears will haunt you. During your quiet time each day, quickly contemplate the thought: *"Is this the way that I want to be thinking and acting? What would Jesus do?"* Make self-reflection a daily habit. Pay close attention to yourself. This is character building.

61

Imagine

Imagine that you can give your family all the money they need.

Imagine that you can give your family all the time with you they need.

Imagine that you will be seen as a respected leader in your community.

Imagine that your students will like you.

Imagine that your employees will work hard for you.

Imagine that people are telling you that you are making a difference in their lives.

Imagine that you can accomplish all you want.

This is not a daydream. This is a result of your being a practicing Catholic following the Action Principles®.

62

Hold Sacred ...

... your Catholic faith.

... your family.

... your good name.

... your given word.

... your moral code.

... your self-reliance.

... your positive attitude.

... your healthy lifestyle.

... your self-improvement.

... your love of learning.

... your willingness to share.

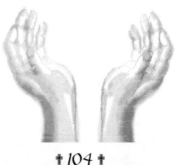

63

Focus on Your Strengths

Rely on your strengths. To know your strengths, you must first acknowledge and then compensate for your weaknesses. Ask your friends and mentors: "*What am I good at? In what areas should I improve?*" What do you do better than most people? Don't be afraid to ask for advice or help and don't be afraid to listen to the answers. Reflect and learn. Knowing yourself allows you to plan your days for peak performance.

In business, solicit comments on your products and services. Customer and employee compliments and complaints are important tools to improve efficiency. Who knows you better?

Accept your limitations. Accept your circumstances.

Following the Catholic Action Principles™, you should have more than enough of everything to succeed. Be the best you can be on the inside, and your beauty and confidence will be reflected on the outside.

64

Understand Courage

There is a difference between physical and moral courage. If you earn a black belt in karate, you may be called upon to be physically courageous but such events will be extraordinary. Even police officers, firemen and military personnel may only have to be physically courageous a few times in their careers.

Moral courage is needed more often than physical courage. Moral courage may mean the challenge to stay with a belief when your position may not be the most popular. Moral courage can be standing tall against bigotry, prejudice, unfairness, and bullying behavior. Moral courage is facing those who may mock your faith. Moral courage is a challenge to do what is right, regardless of the personal consequences. Moral courage may ask you to forgive.

Think of people in physical pain or mental anguish. You may see courage being lived every day.

65

Ask Yourself

Are you healthy enough to keep to a regular exercise schedule?

Are you self-disciplined enough to meet your religious obligations?

Are you smart enough to be able to debate current affairs?

Are you brave enough to take a moral stand?

Are you humble enough to ask for help?

Are you strong enough to delay material gratification?

Are you merciful enough to forgive those who offend you?

Are you generous enough to share your good fortune?

66

Run the Short Road

The short road leads you to physical fitness. If you work out three or four times a week, in three to four months you will probably be in good shape. This is a short road to a notable accomplishment.

The short road leads to financial independence. If you offer a quality product or service and you appreciate your customer and you keep improving, you will earn enough money not to have to worry about it. This is a short road to a notable accomplishment.

The short road leads to strong personal relationships. If you smile at, listen to and are generous with family, employees and the public, you will be rewarded with many friends. If you are courteous, you will be welcomed anywhere. This is a short road to a notable accomplishment.

The short road leads to strong family ties. If parents set the example by adherence to their Catholic faith, insisting on Church attendance and encouraging prayer in the home, they will raise good decision makers. This is a short road to a notable accomplishment.

67

March the Long Road

On the long road, experience beats inexperience; smart beats uninformed; effort beats laziness; polite beats rude; generous beats selfish; fit beats fat and interested beats bored. Be patient. Your time is coming. With time, everything passes from old hands to young.

On the long road, time will reward the prudent investments you make today. An investment in Catholic education will yield a lifetime of benefits.

On the long road, you accept the physical, mental and spiritual blessings that you enjoy from following your Catholic faith as you continue throughout your life to improve yourself and to give back to your family and society.

68

Close the Door on Regrets

The past is only alive if you keep it alive. You can't change yesterday but you can build today for tomorrow. Don't shackle yourself with regrets. Don't start feeling sorry for yourself. Whatever your previous circumstances, others have gotten through the same or worse. Appreciate yourself as a tested survivor, strong and determined. Learn from the past but don't assume that your past automatically equals your future. You are old only when your regrets take the place of your dreams.

Catholics are hopeful. Fill your life with anticipation. Set your goals. Write your to-dos. Just because you haven't done something before doesn't mean that you can't start doing it right now. Be the new, dynamic you. Right now.

69

Avoid Thinking That ...

... you need to chant or fast to find yourself.

... you need a lot of money to start a business.

... you need more than eight hours sleep.

... you need a personal trainer to exercise.

... God would ever give up on you.

... you need advanced university degrees to be successful.

... you need to work forty or fifty years before retirement.

... you need special physical abilities to become an athlete.

... you need more time or resources before helping others.

... you need to criticize more than compliment.

... the world owes you anything.

70

Count the Time

How long does it take to exercise?

How long does it take to stay informed?

How long does it take to be well groomed?

How long does it take to read your child a bedtime story?

How long does it take to say a kind word or deliver a compliment?

How long does it take to clean up after a meal at a shelter?

How long does it take to complete the next entry on your to-do list?

How long does it take to vote?

How long does it take to bring the family to Mass?

Probably just minutes.

71

Act With Boldness

Everyone admires the bold, courageous and daring; no one honors the fainthearted, shy and timid. Look around at what others have done and what you can also do. Everyone is afraid. The strong act in spite of the fear. The weak cower because of the fear. Timidity breeds doubt and hesitation that not only weaken but can be dangerous. The coward dies a thousand deaths.

There is a formula for personal development. It is the same formula for everyone. You must study. You must plan. You must practice. You must be tested. You must be a person of faith. Some will shrink simply facing the task. Some will do the minimum and pass. Some will cut corners and pass. Instead, you must boldly welcome the challenge of honestly meeting the standards. Then and only then will you feel the true pride of accomplishment.

Make a personal decision to do what it will take to succeed. These principles are known to many but lived by few. Most people know what they should be doing. They lack the will or the self-confidence to test themselves physically, mentally and spiritually by starting a business, making an investment, establishing a friendship or raising a family according to Catholic doctrine. You are a person of action.

72

Rejoice In the Day

Psalm 118:24: "This is the day which the Lord hath made; we will rejoice and be glad in it."

You got up early. You did your best at work. You exercised your mind and body. You were pleasant to others. You did a good deed. You took time to reflect and plan tomorrow. You found a small way to spoil yourself. Take pleasure in your accomplishments. Be proud of yourself. If you keep putting days like this together, there is no telling how far you will go and how many lives you will be able to touch in a positive way. Today, you moved one day closer to achieving your goals.

Celebrate small victories and small joys and small wonders. You did your best. Put your head on your pillow. Live vibrantly. Sleep peacefully.

In Loving Memory of H. Woodward LaBossiere

73

Do What You Love Doing

There are 5,000 different types of occupations. Choose one that you love. People have been successful at all of them. They are your models. You can do the same. When you love your job, it doesn't seem like work. If you are caught in dead end employment, use your free time to find a job that you can love doing or start your own business.

There are unlimited activities to occupy your free time. Make sure that each of your days, weeks, months and years are full of activities that you love doing.

Plan to spend a lot of your time doing what you love. You are in control of your own happiness. God is there for you. God wants you to succeed.

74

Appreciate Your Customers

It is people who are going to give you their time, help or money, so you can have everything that you ever wanted in your life for yourself and your family. Those people are voters and tenants and fans and customers and clients and patients and teammates. Listen to them. Appreciate them. Support them. They hold the keys to your success. People who feel appreciated will remain loyal and will become your goodwill ambassadors as they happily sing your praises to others.

By focusing on the needs of others, a wonderful thing happens. You get everything that you want. Customer service is important for the customer, but it is essential to your business. Without customer service, you don't have customers and you don't have a business.

75

Build Networks

You can go a long way by yourself, but you advance much better, much faster, with the help of others. Seek out others with a common purpose and help each other. Join the Knights of Columbus. Get involved in parish activities. Work through your mentors. Find them. Tell them why you admire them. Successful people will not be threatened by your enthusiasm for success. Sincerely ask for their help and often you will be rewarded with positive suggestions and the names of contacts. Carry and exchange business cards. Rehearse a personal introduction that clearly and precisely states who you are and what you do.

Form alliances for common purposes. Establish your own personal support systems. Where do you find good attorneys, physicians, investment advisors, dentists, tailors, or contractors? Ask those you respect for recommendations. If you have a computer, buy a contact management program, and as you meet new people, add them to your personal network database. Keep in regular contact with your network. Form your support systems and personal networks before you need them.

76

Build Your Team

In building your winning team to play a game or build a business, don't be afraid to pick people who are stronger, faster, smarter, better organized, braver, more ambitious, funnier or more pleasant than you are. Ask your best people for recommendations. Think about the spirit on the best teams you were ever on and how your teammates cooperated in reaching a common goal. Think about the dignity and respect your teammates showed to one another. Think about how you were able to rebound from losses to play and win again.

You want your team to be built on excellence. You want your team built with members of merit and character. Resist those who propose membership based upon patronage. Excellence is excellence and is not subject to conditions of race, color, creed, national origin, etc. If people are the best-qualified to fulfill the team's mission, then that's what they are. If they are not, they are not.

77
Negotiate With Power

Almost everything is negotiable. Research and prepare before you meet. Speak with quiet authority. Know what you want and will accept before you begin. Ask for what you want. You shouldn't expect the other party to guess what you want. Be sure that the person you are speaking with can grant your request. Be persistent. Try different angles of attack. Ask the other party to suggest a resolution. Suggest a compromise.

Start the negotiation process with a lower than expected offer. Be reasonable. Don't argue or threaten. Respect the other party's position. Suggest logical arguments for your request. Clearly state your opinion and the repercussions to both parties if an agreement is not reached. When you finalize the sale or negotiate the deal, stop talking, shake hands and move on to a neutral topic.

78

Offer Freely

The single best word in advertising is free. So give freely and reap the rewards.

If you are a hairdresser and need new customers, don't sit in the salon doing nothing. Hand out business cards, give free haircuts and show your expertise.

If you are a black belt, offer free self-defense clinics at factories, schools, fairs and anywhere else that they will let you.

If you are an artist, donate one afternoon a month to teaching at the children's hospital.

Look for ways to say, "free" and keep giving.

When you give with positive intent, you don't have to worry nor should you be worried about the benefits. You will feel good. You will feel appreciated.

There is a universal human law of reciprocity. When you give something to someone, that person feels obligated to give something back. It could be new business. It could be media attention. It could be a testimonial letter. It could be a heart-felt *"Thank you."*

79

Work At Work

Work expands to fill the time available. Many people will work only up to expectations. Some work just hard enough to not get fired. Some people actually work as little as possible at work. No one likes the self-pitying whiner who slinks in the shadows while others do the work. These people create a window of opportunity for you.

Don't worry about being obligated to work more hours to beat the competition. You probably don't have to invest more time. Instead, if you work all the time you are at work, you will probably come out well ahead of your competition. Guard your time; discourage interruptions.

However, don't become lulled into mistaking activity for accomplishment. Follow your prioritized to-do list. Live and appreciate every day as an important day.

80

Learn

You are responsible for your own education – both religious and secular. When you want to learn about a new subject, go to the library. Go to the bookstores and buy books and magazines. Log on to the Internet. Join a club or association. Find experts in the field. Ask questions and more questions. Take courses and ask your teacher questions. Don't just sit there. Make the course your course. As you begin a new subject or reach a new plateau in your studies, there may be awkward and embarrassing moments. Don't be afraid or think that you lack the aptitude to succeed. Everyone goes through the same learning curves. Work to understand the basics. Stick with it.

Hunger for knowledge, because knowledge is power. You don't need to attend famous universities, or burden yourself with piles of college tuition debt. You can learn anything you want to learn. It is a gift that you give yourself. Knowledge is portable. You take it with you everywhere. The smart will defeat the strong.

81

Ask a Lot of Questions

The easiest way to get information is to ask a question and listen to the answer. Good parents, friends, priests, nuns, students and leaders aren't shy. If someone seems upset, depressed or anxious, ask why. Ask and get to the point and you may be able to correct a small incident before it becomes a big problem. If you are rejected, ask a question and you may learn enough to succeed on your next attempt. Let one question lead to the next. Questions are stepping-stones to self-improvement. The only meaningless question is the one not asked.

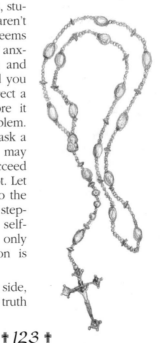

On the receiving side, remember that the truth fears no question.

82

Read Biographies

What if you could learn the success secrets of the greatest people who ever lived? You can.

The lives of the famous and the infamous have been recorded in biographies and are ready for you to read and research.

The lives of great government leaders, businesspeople, humanitarians and saints are there. You will read about successes and triumphs. You will also learn how many times champions and saints lose on their way to winning.

In reading biographies, you may come to the startling conclusion of how much greatness you possess. You may conclude, *"Hey, I can do that."* You can make your life significant. Biographies help show the way. You only have to take the action to go to the library, bookstores or surf the Internet.

83

Be Open to New Ideas

There is always more to learn. Your employees, family, friends, suppliers and even your competitors may all have suggestions that you can put to profitable use.

Be open-minded. Observe, read and listen. Be open to the fact that lots of people are going to have ideas worthy of your consideration. Welcome them. Incorporate the better ideas into your business and personal dealings.

Find new ideas in books, magazines, videos, audiotapes, newsletters, trade literature, and on the Internet. Find new ideas at conventions, seminars, lectures, and by taking evening courses. Seek new experiences and adventures. Who dares wins.

Go to Cathcom.net for a list of Catholic publications that will give you the Catholic perspective on issues.

We must guard against being unchangeable or apathetic.

84

Heed the Warnings

"High voltage." "Wear Your Seat Belt."
"Capacity Limited to 150." "Danger - Thin Ice."
"Don't Drive Drunk."

You may wish that you were invulnerable but
you are not. You are human and your body can
get hurt if you aren't a vigilant guardian of your
own physical safety. Awful accidents may happen
beyond your control. But we are also often fore-
warned. A prudent person appreciates the warn-
ings.

On occasion, you will find yourself in the company of stupid people who don't care about their
own safety or yours. Be courageous. Speak up and
then leave them to their stupidity.

85

Observe and Be Aware

At first, observation and awareness will require conscious effort on your part. Over time, they will become instinctive and will be some of your most valuable skills.

In business, you see ads and get ideas for your ads. You shop in stores and get ideas for your store. There is no point in re-inventing the wheel. If a proven strategy already exists, find it and try it.

In self-defense, you enter a movie theater and you make a mental note of the exits. You walk down an unfamiliar street and automatically scan for the unusual.

In Church, you see strong Catholic families and you see young people making good decisions.

Listen to the speech patterns of powerful people. Be silent. Think twice and speak once. Be an active listener. Look at the person who is talking. Don't interrupt. Be aware of their body language. Listen and they will like you. It is arrogant not to listen. Your self-confidence in mind and body will create a charismatic aura. Ask questions. Stay informed. Get involved. Read newspapers, magazines and books. Watch the news. Fulfill your Catholic obligations.

86

Read, Read, Read

There are few things that we can do that are more important than to instill a love of reading in our children. Reading is a lifelong gift. If you read, you can always educate yourself. It doesn't matter if you are reading from a computer screen, a paperback or from a leather-bound classic. Rather than getting upset at life's delays, A-B-A-B (Always Bring A Book) and put this time to profitable use.

Set the reading example in your home. Children read when they see their parents reading. Keep plenty of books, magazines and newspapers in the house for everyone to read and discuss. Set family reading goals and provide children with incentives for reading. Set aside a time each week for reading aloud as a family. Take regular family trips to bookstores and libraries. Make sure children are involved in a summer reading program. Encourage all family members to give books as presents.

87

Respect and Defend All Life

Who will stand and speak for the children, for the unborn, for the condemned, for those depressed or suffering in physical pain? Defend the rights of the old, lonely, homeless, unwanted, forgotten, the harassed, physically and mentally challenged and depressed. Our blessings morally obligate us to share our time, money and expertise.

The easy course would be indifference and apathy reflected in our silence. When we do not fight for every life, we jeopardize our own. As the twenty-first century dawns, how many alternatives are we willing to consider before we give up even one life? Can we reach out compassionately to those dealing with life issues? Don't we have enough time, talent, money, and love to keep trying?

The strong and brave must defend those who cannot do this themselves. This is leadership. It is preserving human dignity and defending human rights. There, but for the grace of God, go I.

In Loving Memory of Helen and Edward Fagan

88

Honor The Military

As we work toward world peace and we commit to finding nonviolent solutions to our problems, we must acknowledge that our freedom to do so has come as a direct result of those brave men and women who have served in the military. There is no doubt that without a strong response from good, evil would have triumphed. We must remain vigilant in our support of our armed services.

When you hear news of a military engagement, why not pause and say a short prayer for our brave soldiers, sailors, marines and airmen? Say a prayer for their officers and chaplains. Say a prayer for all the combatants and innocents who may be suffering. Pray for peace.

Right now, we can do more. In every city and town there are plaques and street signs to honor those who stood in our places to defend freedom. They left and did not return. They died heroes. They died for us. Yet, we have allowed their memories to fade. School children do not know their stories. We do not know their names. Can you adopt one fallen hero from your town and proclaim his or her name as a hero?

89

Treasure the Earth

We are obligated to future generations to protect our world. Clean air, clean water, green open spaces, national parks and preservation of our natural resources are everyone's business. Human beings are dependent creatures. Each of us must accept responsibility and do our part. We can be active supporters. We can pick up litter in parks and streets without worrying how it got there. We can recycle and be aware of the disposability of the products we buy. We can plant trees. With mindful attention, we thank God for these wonderful gifts he has given us.

Others will notice our example. Educators and parents must join together to teach environmental awareness to our youngsters and, by example, the importance of conservation. Tread softly. Be mindful of the fragility of our planet.

90

Allow Your Opponent To Save Face

In business, sport or everyday relations, always allow your opponent to save face. You won. That should be enough. Bragging is counterproductive – you simply present the opportunity for your audience to think the opposite. It costs little for you to offer your opponent the opportunity to excuse his loss. In fact, you may gain appreciation from many observers.

To taunt or shame a defeated opponent may simply set the stage for another confrontation, with the odds stacked against you. Your humiliated opponent may plot to redeem his lost honor by staging a rematch with more allies and more powerful weapons. You turn a quick battle into a long-term war.

If you lose, do so with grace and good spirit. You won't always win, but you can always respond as a good Catholic and do what you believe to be right. For you, there will be another day. If you win, be gracious in victory, because some day very soon you will be vulnerable. Winning provides you with the opportunity to show both mercy and humility.

91

Thank Your Ancestors

Learning is a process of self-discovery. Usually, that self-discovery is based on the trial and error and experience of those who have come before us. Someone ventured forth from the safe warmth of the prehistoric campfire. Someone hankered for a better life overseas. The curiosity and bravery of others has given us the knowledge to live long, comfortable lives. The human race is stronger and more adaptable today than ever before. Whatever you hope to accomplish with your life, the going will be easier because of the hard work and chances taken by those who came before us.

Be grateful to the saints who have defined our Catholic faith. Be grateful for the explorers and scientists. Be grateful for all teachers who pass the love and enthusiasm for their subjects to us. Be grateful to your parents. Be grateful to your personal mentors. Be grateful to anyone who took a personal interest in you.

Continue down the path. Respect those who work on your behalf. Some day, you will be old and will appreciate the repayment of others' kindness. Thank your ancestors.

92

Practice Peace

Peace begins within each of us. We find it in our quiet time in personal reflection. We find it in the examples of our saints and clergy. It is shown in the understanding and forgiveness that we extend to each other. We can only teach peace by becoming examples of peace. Being peaceful, we extend peace to all we encounter. Peace is not a distant ideal but right here, right now.

Peace is not born from weakness. We must practice peace. As people of action, we must assume the mantle of defenders of the peace. We must remain vigilant and ready, willing and able to take the action to protect those in our neighborhoods victimized by bullies. Enemies of peace must never be appeased through our apathy or encouraged by our indecisiveness.

93

Make Everyone Feel Important

Teach with enthusiasm and your love for your subject will spread. Sell your products or services with enthusiasm and your company will grow. Presume that your students and employees and customers are your equals because they are. Don't teach or sell down to anyone. Speak with and not at or to your students or customers. Learn and use peoples' names.

Make everyone you meet feel important. You can't be selectively likable. If you try to like some people and not others, you will eventually be seen as a phony, and no one wants to do business with a phony.

When you talk down to people, you shift the focus from your subject or product to your condescending attitude.

Listen. Be patient. Pay attention. Don't interrupt or fidget. Make eye contact. Smile and nod encouragement. Don't try to top another's story with your own heroic tales.

People love to be involved in projects which they helped design. Help others to identify and develop their strengths. Be quick to praise and slow to criticize. Look for opportunities to teach others about the Catholic faith.

94

Give Generously

Follow the Catholic faith and you will be blessed with much more than you need. You will work hard toward your goals and you will be liked. Just these two attributes will result in your being well rewarded. Your organizational abilities will allow you to have more time than most. Your persistence and determination will get you more financial reward than most. You must earn before you can give. Share your time and money. Send lots of flowers, candy, e-mails, handwritten cards, teddy bears and thank yous. Extend a helping hand. Smile. Compliment. Tell jokes. Laugh. Remember names, anniversaries and birthdays. Be generous and then forget it. Your example will be one that others will admire, respect and follow.

Selflessly share your time and money because it is right. You will set in motion a chain of positive actions and reactions. To be unselfish, sharing, generous, bountiful, magnanimous, noble-minded and gracious is much more about attitude than about money. As much as you give, much more will you receive.

95

Share the Credit

If you organize a group to clean up a park, let everyone enjoy the thank yous. If your sports team wins a competition or makes a good showing, be proud, step back and let everyone walk around with the trophy.

If your sales team meets its objectives or if your customer service department solves a tough problem, take everyone out to lunch. Let everyone laugh.

As a leader, your greatest satisfaction should come from seeing the people in your team, department or company succeed. Share the credit and experience the camaraderie. You know who you are. Let others glow in the feeling of accomplishing a mutual goal. Be enthusiastic for others. Acknowledge exceptional work. Encourage cooperation. Your reward will be many friends.

Are we ready to say, *"Yes, we can do more. Yes, we can give more."*?

In Loving Memory of John and Jean Hazelton

137

96

Promote The Catholic Action Principles™

The Catholic Action Principles™ are yours. Toss this book into your pocket, purse or pack and when you have a free moment, read a principle. The surest way for you to stay on your personal journey to peace and prosperity is to get involved. All the work that you do for us helps others and reinforces your own commitment to success.

Take action. Spread the word and help us help others. You can tell co-workers and friends about the Catholic Action Principles™. Send them to Success.org to learn more. You can give a copy of this book to someone you care about. You can check that the public and school libraries in your town have copies of this book. If you are able, purchase and donate copies of the book to social or educational organizations. Most importantly, you can be the example. Share your success and your knowledge.

97

Walk The Talk

When you live your life with concern and love for others as a practicing Catholic, wonderful things will happen. You will be fulfilled. You will feel a warm pride from your selfless acts that will then allow you the grace of humility. To be first, you must put yourself last. The true leader goes to the end of the line. Say what you mean and mean what you say. Be sure your words match your deeds.

Can you give a dollar to a beggar? Can you lend an ear to one avoided by others? Can you work an extra shift for a parent who needs to be with a sick child? Can you visit a shut-in? Can you speak up and defend a poor soul being teased or bullied? Can you treat all people as your brothers and sisters? Your example may become contagious.

As Mother Teresa taught us, the greatest sorrow is to be lonely and unloved. Refuse to let this happen with your idle consent. Right now, the days of homelessness, hunger and unsafe streets can be relieved if we make the commitment.

98

Teach Our Children...

... a respect for all life.

... the benefits of hard work and frugality.

... the value of physical fitness and healthy living.

... the merits of military and public service.

... the importance of charity and volunteering.

... a pride in heritage, home and country.

... the advantages of courtesy and manners.

... the power of knowledge.

... the blessings of positive thinking.

... the strength in self-reliance.

... the goodness of man.

... faith in God.

... the joys of fully living our Catholic faith.

Children will only learn from us as we become the example.

99

Be A Mentor

If you want to learn first hand about a new subject and drastically shorten the learning curve, one of the best ways is to find a mentor. A mentor is an experienced person who is doing or has done what it is that you want to do and agrees to be your guide. Many successful people remember their own early struggles and gladly agree to serve as mentors, especially if you are an enthusiastic, appreciative novice. Besides sharing their knowledge, some mentors offer the additional bonus of sharing their contacts and networks. Imagine being able to consult with a senior partner who has been there and done that and whom you don't have to pay.

As others are willing to help you, don't forget your own potential role as mentor. Offer your services as a CCD teacher or CYO coach. Even a small amount of time can make a big difference to a newcomer. Listen for the wise words of experience.

In Loving Memory of Anthony and Elizabeth Unanue

100

Call to Action

It is the people who make a country great. In every country, brave, compassionate people of action must be willing to assume the mantle of leadership and face the challenges to religion, education, law, government, health care, the environment and human rights. If you live the Catholic faith, this person is you. Even as one, your example can make a difference. Your strong moral stance can give courage to the many who may face the relentless evil intent of a few. You will not be alone. The Catholic faith is over one billion strong and growing.

This is a call to action. Following the Catholic faith will show you the clear path to peace and prosperity in your life and beyond. Live the faith with your family. Pass it on.

Mother Teresa

Mother Teresa (1910-1997). Indian (Albanian-born) humanitarian and missionary; a charismatic and tireless worker, she founded the Order of the Missionaries of Charity whose mission was to love and care for the unwanted. She was awarded the Nobel Peace Prize in 1979. In her words:

MOTHER TERESA

The most terrible poverty is loneliness and the feeling of being unloved.

✝

God doesn't require us to succeed; he only requires that you try.

✝

If you can't feed a hundred people, then feed just one.

✝

Let no one ever come to you without leaving better and happier.

✝

We can do no great things; only small things with great love.

✝

If you judge people, you have no time to love them.

✝

Kind words can be short and easy to speak, but their echoes are truly endless.

✝

Smile at each other, make time for each other in your family.

✝

Saint Elizabeth Ann Seton

Saint Elizabeth Ann Seton (1774-1821). An impoverished widow with five children, Mother Seton supported her children by opening a Catholic girls' school in Baltimore. Mother Seton's work was the beginning of the parochial school system in America. To run the school system she founded the Sisters of Charity, the first native American religious community for women. In her words:

SAINT ELIZABETH ANN SETON

O Father, the first rule of Our dear Savior's life was to do Your Will. Let His Will of the present moment be the first rule of our daily life and work, with no other desire but for its most full and complete accomplishment. Help us to follow it faithfully, so that doing what You wish we will be pleasing to You. Amen.

✝

We must pray without ceasing, in every occurrence and employment of our lives - that prayer which is rather a habit of lifting up the heart to God as in a constant communication with Him.

✝

We know certainly that our God calls us to a holy life. We know that he gives us every grace, every abundant grace; and though we are so weak of ourselves, this grace is able to carry us through every obstacle and difficulty.

Saint Vincent de Paul

Saint Vincent (1581-1660), together with St. Louise de Marillac, founded hospitals and orphanages, opened soup kitchens, created job training programs, bettered prison conditions, and organized charities throughout France. In his words:

SAINT VINCENT DE PAUL

Let us love God my brothers, let us love God. But let it be with the strength of our arms and the sweat of our brow.

✝

Serve the poor, you lose nothing, since to serve the poor is to go to God. You must see God in the faces of the poor.

✝

We should assist the poor in every way, and do it both by ourselves and by enlisting the help of others.

✝

What! To be a Christian and see a Brother afflicted without weeping with him, without being sick with him, would be to be without charity, to be a mere picture of a Christian, to be without humanity, to be worse than brute beasts!

✝

Love is inventive, even to infinity.

✝

Give me persons of prayer and they will be capable of anything.

✝

Saint Ignatius Loyola

Saint Ignatius of Loyola (1491-1556) was a soldier turned pilgrim turned priest. His meditations, prayers, visions and insights led to the founding of the Jesuits. Today, the Jesuit community comprises 30,000 members with 500 universities serving 200,000 students.

SAINT IGNATIUS
LOYOLA

PRAYER OF SAINT IGNATIUS LOYOLA

Teach us to be generous, good Lord;

Teach us to serve You as You deserve;

To give and not to count the cost;

To fight and not to heed the wounds;

To toil and not to seek for rest;

To labor and not ask for any reward

Save that of knowing that we do Your will.

✝

Saint Francis of Assisi

*Saint Francis of Assisi (1181-1226).
Son of a wealthy merchant, after living a
pampered youth, he was converted to a
higher calling. He dressed in cast-off
clothing and begged for his simple needs.
He lived with animals, cared for lepers
and worked with his hands. He visited
hospitals, served the sick, preached in the
streets, and took all men and women as
siblings. Founder of the Franciscan Friars, he was a man of
action who preached peace.*

SAINT FRANCIS
OF ASSISI

PRAYER OF SAINT FRANCIS OF ASSISI

Lord, make me an instrument of your peace.
Where there is hatred, let me sow love;
where there is injury, pardon; where there is doubt, faith;
where there is despair, hope; where there is darkness, light;
and where there is sadness, joy.

O Divine Master, grant that I may not so much seek
to be consoled as to console;
to be understood as to understand; to be loved as to love.
For it is in giving that we receive;
it is in pardoning that we are pardoned;
and it is in dying that we are born to eternal life. Amen

Saint Augustine of Hippo

Saint Augustine of Hippo (354-430). A wild youth converted through the prayers of his mother, Saint Monica. Selling all of his possessions, he gave all of his money to the poor and founded a monastery. He was a monk, priest, preacher, founder of religious communities and later Bishop of Hippo. He was a Doctor of the Church known for his rhetoric and writing. In his words:

SAINT AUGUSTINE OF HIPPO

God has no need of your money, but the poor have. You give it to the poor, and God receives it.

✝

This very moment I may, if I desire, become the friend of God.

✝

God bestows more consideration on the purity of the intention with which our actions are performed than on the actions themselves.

✝

Conquer yourself and the world lies at your feet.

✝

The honors of this world, what are they but puff, and emptiness and peril of falling?

✝

Daily advance, then, in this love, both by praying and by well doing, that through the help of Him who enjoined it on you, and whose gift it is, it may be nourished and increased, until, being perfected, it render you perfect.

✝

What will I be?

Everyone is called to be with God,
whether married, single, clergy or religious.

Some people are called to be with God
as a priest, brother or sister.

It is not a calling to do anything,
go anywhere, or become something.

It is a call to a state of being.

Are you being called?

ReligiousMinistries.com

Write Your
Catholic Action Principle

We need your experience, knowledge and insights to make the Catholic Action Principles™ truly representative of our faith and the example we all endeavor to set.

Your Catholic Action Principle™ should be between 80 and 200 words and written in the third person. The best principles are focused, action-oriented, inspirational and each represents a single Catholic theme. Add a short action-oriented title. Original illustrations and photos appropriate to the principle are welcome. Use the online form to submit your work.

Teachers are encouraged to have their classes write a collective Catholic Action Principle™ as a project. All appropriate submissions will be posted on Success.org.

Translators Needed

We need translators willing to volunteer their skills to bring the Catholic Action Principles™ to the world as a free ebook. Acknowledgement for your work will be posted on Success.org to accompany your translation.

The American
Success Institute

The American Success Institute [ASI] is a 501[c]3 non-profit educational and philanthropic organization founded in 1993 by Bill FitzPatrick. The mission of ASI is to create a worldwide community in which all members are fully involved participants living and encouraging the expansion of the Action Principle® ideals of self-improvement and service based on established religious faith.

SUCCESS.org

Success.org is ASI's multi-media interactive website featuring free courses on business and personal development. Students visiting the site will find resource materials, discussion forums and ways to join us in our work.

Many national and world leaders have contributed to our Action Principles® Leadership Project.

Join Us
The Catholic Action Principles Project

"I sense that the moment has come to commit all of the Church's energies to a new evangelization ..." – Pope John Paul II.

Who could be helped receiving a copy of this book?

- † A person in moral anguish.
- † A teacher preparing lesson plans.
- † A family sharing positive dinner conversation.
- † A teenager facing a tough decision.
- † A counselor leading a support group.
- † A lapsed Catholic finding reasons to return to the Church.

Be an angel. Join us in defraying the cost of printing and distributing the Catholic Action Principles™. Whether you can afford a single line remembrance or a full-page sponsorship, your donation is needed and appreciated. Investments in this evangelical project begin at only $100. Your contribution will be represented as a permanent acknowledgement in tens of thousands of printed books and, also, as perpetual online memorialization. You may never know who might pick up a copy of YOUR book. You may never know, but God will. Complete details on Catholic ActionPrinciples.com or by calling 800-585-1300.

Become an Catholic Action Principles Champion™

Be the Motivator in Service to Others

It will always be the obligation of the strong to help and protect those less fortunate. If you feel blessed and believe in the positive spirit of the Action Principles®, please join us by becoming a Catholic Action Principles Champion™. Some of our work:

- Empowering millions around world to lead more productive and peaceful lives through our free courses and e-books on Success.org
- Donating tens of thousands of books to schools and social agencies
- Assisting humanitarian missions with special service to those in uniform

As a Catholic Action Principles Champion™, you will receive recognition awards and signed books and posters. But more importantly, at your option, on a regular and recurring basis, you will receive an assortment of motivational materials to share with family and others in your community. Distributing these gifts of hope, you will be the motivator.

Respect and appreciation will be yours as a Catholic Action Principles Champion™. Even if no one ever learns of your contribution, you will know. Those who you help will know. God will know. This is the path to bringing peace and prosperity into your own life. Thank you.

Become A Catholic Action Principles Champion™

$15 per month - Less than 50 cents a day. Details on our Champion, Grand Champion, World Champion and Donor Programs on CatholicActionPrinciples.com or call 800-585-1300

Catholic Websites
Study – Practice – Teach

Vatican.va _____ Official Vatican website

NewAdvent.org _____ Encyclopedia, resources & links

EWTN.com _____ TV, radio and Mother Angelica

Catholic.com _____ Catholic answers

Catholic.org _____ News, forums, prayers & more

Catholic.net _____ News, The Pope, bookstore and more

AmericanCatholic.org ___ Franciscan perspective

Usccb.org _____ American Church hierarchy

Catholic-forum.com ___ Find your patron saint

Catholicexchange.com _ Supersite with resources, links

Catholic-extension.org _ American missions

StRaphael.net _____ Catholic singles

CIN.org _____ Catholic Information Network

KofC.org _____ Knights of Columbus

CUA.edu _____ Catholic University of America

STAC.edu _____ St. Thomas Aquinas College

Vincenter.org _____ The Vincentian Center

FranciscanFriars.com ___ Father Groeschel and more

Catholiccollegesonline.org __ Catholic colleges

Schalifax.ca _____ Sisters of Charity of Halifax

Catholic Action Package $50

Order the Catholic Action Package $50

- 5 Copies of the Catholic Action Principles™
- Master Success (the book)
- Positive Mental Attitudes
- Sports Legends on Success
- African-Americans on Success
- 10 Action Principle® Posters

To order:

Online: CatholicActionPrinciples.com/order
Phone: 1-800-585-1300
Fax: 508-653-2924
Email: orders@CatholicActionPrinciples.com
Mail: American Success Institute
5 North Main St.
Natick, MA 01760

About Bill FitzPatrick

Bill FitzPatrick is a teacher. Through his work, Bill hopes to instill in his students a greater appreciation of their potential to live happy, prosperous lives of service. Bill lives with his wife Karen in a Boston suburb. Bill and Karen are the proud aunt and uncle to many wonderful nieces and nephews.

BILL FITZPATRICK

Bill Teaches on Success.org

Bill teaches free online courses on small business, real estate, personal performance and self-defense. New students with a commitment to self-improvement and helping others are always welcomed to study and add their insights.

SUCCESS.org

Together We Can

Let's start our own positive conversations. You are important to us. Your ideas and impressions of this book are important to us. Working together, we can make the *Catholic Action Principles*™ a more effective personal reflection, conversation, teaching and evangelism tool.

How did you get your copy of the *Catholic Action Principles*™? What do you like about the book? What changes would you suggest? Would you recommend the book? Would you give the book as a gift? Would you feel comfortable sharing the book with a lapsed Catholic or a non-Catholic? How do you use the book? What creative ideas do you have for other individuals or groups to benefit from these positive thoughts?

We are interested in your stories and testimonials. How have the *Catholic Action Principles*™ made a positive impact on your life or someone else's? Tell us. If you have Internet access, please go to http://Success.org/Survey and take our survey. Or, join the online Discussion Forum. Thank you for your input. We appreciate it!

Special Offer

Evangelize!

Be an Angel!

Share with:
Family
Friends
Students
Co-workers
Parish

100 books $100 + $25 shipping

Bonus Books Free

You will also receive: Positive Mental Attitudes
• Master Success Sports Legends on Success •
African-Americans on Success
$37 value **free!**

Educational, nonprofit and clergy discount of
10%=$115 total.

To Order Online: CatholicActionPrinciples.com/order
Phone: 800-585-1300
Fax: 508-653-2924
Email: orders@CatholicActionPrinciples.com
Mail: ASI, 5 N Main St., Natick, MA 01760

Let's Begin

Choosing to live your life as a practicing Catholic, committed to improving yourself and helping others, you may start anywhere and there is no telling where you will end up. This is your glorious life's journey. Let your Catholic faith and the guidance of these Action Principles® lead you to write your goals, make your plans, list your to-dos and make today and every day special. Live a full, rich, rewarding life. Inspire others by your quiet example. At the end of the day, you can relax. You'll be tired, but satisfied and happy that you have done your best. You will be smiling and so will God.

Be the best that you can be because you can't conceive of living any other way. Stand tall. You will be surrounded by genuine affection from your husband, wife, children, friends and co-workers. Even strangers will react positively to you, having sensed your confidence. Love, friendship, respect, peace and prosperity will be yours to live and enjoy every day. In trying, you are a master of success. This may all seem miraculous to you but it will just be you following God's plan.

See you at CatholicActionPrinciples.com

Bill